THE $EVEN W!NNING NUMBERS

Your path to creating wealth with certainty
(leave nothing to chance)

DREW PARTRIDGE CFP®

First Edition — 2023

Copyright © Ridgeback Investments Pty Ltd 2023

All rights reserved.

No part of this publication may be reproduced, stored, or transmitted in any form by any means without the written permission from the author. It is illegal to copy this book, post it to a website or distribute it by any other means without permission. This book is copyright.

All names, characters, examples and events mentioned in this book are fictitious. No identification with actual persons, places or products should be inferred.

Drew Partridge asserts the moral right to be identified as the author of this book.

ISBN: 978-0-646-87017-5 (paperback)
ISBN: 978-0-646-87018-2 (eBook)

A catalogue record for this book is available from the National Library of Australia.

Illustrator — Gary Wells
Graphic Designer — Tess McCabe

www.ridgebackfinancialplanning.com.au

Disclaimer

The information in this book is general in nature only. It does not represent professional or personal advice, and should not be relied upon as the basis for any decision to take (or not take) action on any topic mentioned in the book.

Before making any financial decisions, you should consult a licensed financial adviser who will take into account your own financial objectives, personal situation and needs.

No warranty is given as to the accuracy, reliability or completeness of information contained in this book. The author does not accept any liability for any error or omission in the book, or for any loss or damage suffered by any person as a result.

The products referred to in this book are included for illustration purposes only, and are neither a recommendation, nor an endorsement.

When considering any financial product, you should obtain and read the relevant Product Disclosure Statement carefully, to assess whether the product is appropriate for your circumstances. Always conduct your own research, before making any financial and/or investment decision.

As an investor, Drew Partridge may hold a financial interest in funds, companies or investments mentioned in this book.

The author is not associated with any financial entity and receives no commissions, 'backhanders' or financial rewards for talking about any product or brand in this book. No such arrangements exist.

For Lance Corporal Tyrone Barrass

45 Commando, Royal Marines

We all joined the Marines looking for something. We weren't sure if we would find what we were looking for whilst serving, but we joined up and served anyway.

In Afghanistan, we were scathing of the Taliban. But they had actually found what they were looking for and we were the ones still searching.

I wish you had found what you were looking for before your life was taken.

Rest well my friend.

You have not been forgotten.

ABOUT THE AUTHOR

Drew Partridge is a Certified Financial Planner® and runs his own independent financial planning practice: Ridgeback Financial Planning. He has over 11 years of experience in the finance sector as a financial planner and in business banking.

Drew is also a former Royal Marine and served as a Special Forces Communicator attached to the Special Boat Service, completing four tours of duty.

He studied Business at the Queensland University of Technology, majoring in Economics. He also holds an Advanced Diploma in Financial Planning. Drew is a member of the Financial Planning Association of Australia.

Drew completed the high watermark qualification for the Australian financial planning industry in 2019: the Certified Financial Planner® Designation through the Financial Planning Association of Australia.

He lives with his wife Rhian and son in the Gold Coast hinterland, and loves to train and participate in masters' rowing regattas in his spare time.

CONTENTS

Disclaimer ii
About the author v
Introduction 1

PART 1: Establishing Your Financial Foundation

Chapter 1: The fundamentals 6
   Winning the lotto 6
   The 'haves' versus the 'have-nots' 7
   Financial freedom and success 9

Chapter 2: The Seven Winning Numbers 12
   Winning Number 3: Managing your cash flow 14
      Step 1: Open up your 3 bank accounts 16
      Step 2: Calculate your fixed expenses and
      set up a direct debit 17
   Winning Number 20: Saving 21
      Step 3: Save 21
      Step 4: Spend and have fun! 23
      Debt — Take control of your debt and stop
      it controlling you! 29
      Car loans 32
      Credit cards — Should I have one? 34
      Credit cards and fraud 35
      Defaulting on debt 37

Winning Number 55: The 'Danger Zone' 39
Winning Number 4: Paying your mortgage off faster 45
    Strategy 1: Paying fortnightly 45
    Strategy 2: Making extra repayments. 46
    Strategy 3: An offset account. 46
    Strategy 4: Refinancing your home loan 48
    Using a mortgage calculator 49
Winning Number 10: Finding another 10% savings 52
Winning Number 5: An extra 5% a day keeps the
    doctor away 55
If you're self-employed 61
Winning Number 120: How to invest
    your superannuation. 62
The rule of 120: Take the number 120 and subtract
    your age 64
The Seven Winning Numbers again 67

PART 2: Building On Your Solid Financial Foundations

Chapter 3: Investing and building wealth 71
Compound interest 71
Investing in the share market 75
    Listed investment companies (LICs) 78
    Unlisted actively managed funds 79
    Exchange traded funds (EFTs) 80
    Diversification. 83
Fear and greed. 94
A sound approach to buying shares. 95
Your circle of trust 98
Whose name should you invest in? 100
Insurance bonds 101
Investing in residential property 103
Cryptocurrencies 106
The greater fool theory. 109

Chapter 4: Gearing (borrowing to invest) 110
- Negative gearing versus positive gearing 114
  - Negative gearing.................................. 114
  - Positive gearing................................... 115
- Margin lending.. 117

Chapter 5: Trade-offs 120
- Paying off your mortgage faster versus contributing more to super 120
  - Crunching the numbers scenario.................. 121
- Paying off the home loan faster versus investing outside of super........................ 123

Chapter 6: Estate planning 127
- Your key estate planning areas...................... 128
  - Drawing up a will............................... 128
  - Enduring power of attorney form 131
  - Death benefit nominations for your superannuation . 131
  - Life insurance beneficiary nominations 132

Chapter 7: Insurance 135
- Personal insurance.................................. 135
- Your most valuable financial asset................... 137
  - Life insurance 139
  - Trauma insurance 139
  - Total and permanent disability (TPD) 139
  - Income protection 140
- How much insurance do I need? 141
- Reviewing your personal insurance................... 142
- Applying for personal insurance 143
- Compromising on cost versus benefit................. 144
  - Health insurance 145
- General insurance and purchasing a car 149

Chapter 8: Being self-employed. 152
    Separating yourself from your business 152
    Superannuation 155
    Self-managed super funds (SMSF)
        and commercial premises. 155
    Business expenses insurance. 159

PART 3: Applying the Winning Numbers

Scenario 1: Young adult. 163
Scenario 2: Young family. 172
Scenario 3: Middle-aged couple with teenage children 186

Epilogue: Sleepwalking 204
Conclusion 207
Helpful websites and resources. 209
Supporting the environment. 211
Endnotes 214

Introduction

Not all of us choose a career path that pays well. The employment market is not always fair; those who contribute most to the greater good, are often paid substantially less than those who do not.

Whether we like it or not, talent will be drawn to occupations that pay the best. For example, thousands of boys around the world aspire to be a Premier League soccer player. And if they make it into the big time, they can be paid on average three million pounds sterling — per year — just to kick a ball around a grass pitch.[1]

I find it somewhat distasteful that these soccer players often cheat by faking injury, simply to gain a penalty advantage. Not only is this behaviour acceptable to the player, it is expected of them by their employer. They are financially incentivised to cheat, in order to win.

Yet a school teacher who helps prepare children for the future, or a paramedic who saves the lives of car crash victims day after day, will take years to earn what a top soccer player makes in just a couple of months.

If you think about it, in the few minutes that a Premier League player rolls around on the grass pretending to have been shot, he has earned more than you will earn this week. Such is life, and such is the employment market.

However, there is no need to aspire to be filthy, stinking rich. Becoming a billionaire does not guarantee happiness, but worrying about money does destroy happiness.

Having the financial means to enjoy life (both while you are working and in retirement) contributes handsomely to you being happy and content: you can spend more time with your loved ones, and do more of the things in life that you enjoy.

As Australians, we are already fortunate to have been born in a safe, democratic and developed country with a good rule of law. When I conducted my tours of duty in Afghanistan, I saw the exact opposite — especially for women.

The life of an Afghan is not a life you would want to experience. There is little opportunity to succeed and get ahead. Humans can be very cruel, and I found it bewildering that a culture could survive with such intolerance and barbaric traditions. In comparison, we live in a society that allows most of us to succeed, and achieve our full potential.

The purpose of this book is to help people who have chosen a career path based primarily on passion and fulfillment, rather than one paying an income that guarantees great wealth. When concerted effort is put into both your career and into creating wealth, you can achieve your full potential not only personally, but also financially.

When considering my approach to writing this book, the first decision I made was not to sit on the fence. I have always found it frustrating when financial commentators talk about the next financial opportunity, or reveal a new financial 'revelation', but then talk about it in a vague or inconclusive manner. They are intentionally unclear, of course, because if they are wrong they don't want to look foolish. When you think about it, they are there mainly as a form of entertainment.

How often do you sit there, after listening to someone talk about money, and ask yourself, "Ok, so that's what I should be doing with my money, but how do I actually do that?"

The second decision I made was not to write about anything that I would not do myself, have not already done, or am not doing currently. In this book you will find fundamental principles on how to manage money in real life — that actually work. No nonsense.

I am acutely aware of the low level of trust people have in financial planners. I found the cultural difference between the military and the financial planning environment confronting. The military unit I served in valued integrity highly. A lack of it saw you moved back to your original unit — fast.

In financial planning, it is often how much money you make out of a client that counts, not how sound your advice is. When it comes to dealing with people's money (if left unchecked) profit is readily prioritised over ethical virtue. From experience, it pays to be cautious.

Contained in this book is a comprehensive financial framework that will enable you to enjoy life today, and at the same time prepare for an enjoyable retirement tomorrow. A framework that will help you build the financial resources to do the things that bring fun, joy and fulfillment at all stages of your life.

This is a book you can read at your own pace and multiple times, to reflect on its key points. You can write notes all over the pages, highlight bits, and discuss its contents with others before taking (or not taking) any action. This book contains sound financial knowledge in black and white. You can take it or leave it.

PART 1
Establishing your financial foundation

CHAPTER 1
The fundamentals

Winning the lotto

I have met many people who play the lotto (or the lottery) religiously every week. They see it as the way to make all their money worries disappear. In one fell swoop, their financial struggles would be over. The hope, the thrill, and the thought of a big win, drives people to keep taking a chance.

One day our numbers will come up. It's only a matter of time!

So, what are the actual chances of winning the lotto?

- The chance of winning Powerball is 1 in 134,490,400.
- The chance of winning Oz Lotto is 1 in 62,891,499.
- The chances of winning the Monday, Wednesday or Saturday lotto is 1 in 8,145,060.

If you don't believe me, you can view these statistics for yourself on *The Lott* website![2] With these odds, chances are you will be dead before your numbers come up.

I see people taking this same approach to the share market, as well as life in general. They have a lottery mindset. They dabble in the share market, taking uneducated risks because they believe a big win is their only hope. They are looking for that pot of gold to make all their financial worries go away.

For some, they want to avoid years of hard work and thrift. For others, they are just not where they want to be in life, and want to catch up. They look with envy at their friends, who may be doing better.

The 'haves' versus the 'have-nots'

Why is it that you can have two people who:

- both have the same job,
- earn the same income, and
- go through the same ups and downs in life, and yet one of them ends up financially much better off — without working any harder?

Was it because they won the lotto?

Was it because they left it to chance?

No! It is because that person planned to be financially better off.

They:

- saved some of their wage,
- invested their savings carefully,
- had adequate personal insurance in place to protect themselves,
- made extra contributions to superannuation, and
- paid off their home loan faster than they needed to.

They didn't leave it to chance. They weren't chasing that 'pot of gold'. They did not have a lotto mindset.

But over time their numbers did come up, and they won! However, the numbers I'm talking about are not related to hope, and they certainly don't involve playing the lotto.

Financial freedom and success

> *"Wealth is the ability to fully experience life."*
> — *Henry David Thoreau (philosopher)*

Think about what financial success means to you. Does it mean:

- being free of money worries?
- being able to send your kids to private school?
- being debt-free?
- an early retirement?
- travelling overseas for a holiday every year?

Pause for a moment and write down what financial success means to you.

_____
_____
_____

So, what does financial success mean for me, you might ask?

Well, for me it means being totally free from debt, and building up several sources of income that will fund my retirement comfortably, and with absolute certainty.

In doing so, I can do whatever I want, whenever I want in retirement.

I don't just want to hope that I will be financially successful!

I want to know with *certainty*!

Why several sources of income?

If the returns from one investment are impacted by something unexpected, then I will still have income from other sources.

What am I talking about when I say sources of income?

I'm talking about:
- superannuation,
- a rental property,
- a managed investment fund, and
- a share portfolio.

I do not intend to work any longer than I have to. I know plenty of things I'd love to do that do not involve working. I want to be able to travel, go camping, see more of Australia, play sport, tend the garden, and spend time with my family and friends.

Let's go back to what you have written down. Take a look again.

Much of what you have written will take money to make it happen. That's just life.

And life if you want to live it, costs money.

So, how are you going to get from where you are now, to where you want to be financially?

The lotto?

Just by chance?

No little grasshopper, you're not!

You will discover the framework to manage your financial life in this book. A framework that will give you a sense of control over your money, a sense of direction, and a sense of confidence that you are heading for financial success with certainty!

You need to be in control of your money.

You need to stop worrying about money.

You need to know that your hard work and effort now will one day be rewarded.

Once you apply this framework to managing your money, you can then focus on the more important things like family, friends, career, travel, and fun. Don't let money hold you back from living your life.

Many people don't think they need to plan what they do with their money. Let me say this: a fool with a plan will beat a genius with no plan.

And a genius with a plan?

Well, you show me.

CHAPTER 2

The Seven Winning Numbers

No, these are not the numbers you play the lotto with. Do you remember what the chances of picking those winning numbers are? These are The Seven Winning Numbers for betting on *you*. And the chance of you winning with these numbers is 1 in 1.

This chapter will explain how you can use The Seven Winning Numbers to do each of the following, in order to set yourself up for financial success with certainty:

- Put your hard-earned income to good use.
- Save for emergencies.
- Clear any bad debt you may have.
- Pay off your home loan faster.
- Avoid the 'Danger Zone'.
- Invest for the future.
- Get your superannuation working harder for you.

You will also learn about the insurances you need to have in place to protect you and your family from financial hardship, what insurances you don't need, and how to play the insurance 'game' to your advantage. If you are self-employed, there are pointers on how to better reward yourself for the additional risk you take on while running your own business.

So, why would you undertake this journey and bet on the Seven Winning Numbers?

Because financially, the best person to look after you when you are old, is you when you are young.

Let us begin by briefly explaining each of The Seven Winning Numbers. We will then explain each Winning Number in more detail.

Winning Number 3
Establish 3 bank accounts to manage your hard-earned income and put it to good use.

Winning Number 20
Save 20 per cent of your income to clear any bad debt you may have accumulated, build an emergency fund, and then invest.

Winning Number 55
Aim to be mortgage-free by the time you are 55 so that you do not enter the 'Danger Zone' with home loan debt.

Winning Number 4
Take 4 steps to pay off your home loan as fast as humanly possible.

Winning Number 10
Save an additional 10 per cent and use those savings to make extra repayments on your home loan.

Winning Number 5
Salary sacrifice 5 per cent of your pre-tax salary into your superannuation fund, save on tax and make your super savings grow faster.

Winning Number 120
Invest your superannuation savings according to your age and life stage with the Rule of 120, and make your super savings work harder.

Winning Number 3: Managing your cash flow

I had a client once who rang me perplexed. He told me he was going through his monthly budget allowance in 2½ weeks. So, I asked him to send me his credit card and bank statements for the last full month.

I then asked him if that last full month was a typical month for his family expenses.

He confirmed it was.

I went through his statements line by line. I chose three expense amounts that stood out. I then multiplied each amount by 12.

Looking at what you spend in a year is important, it adds perspective.

The three items I chose amounted to (rounded):
1. $16,000 a year on takeaway food and eating out,
2. $8,500 a year on take-away coffees, and
3. $5,500 a year on technology for all family members (i.e., mobile phones, internet/wi-fi, pay TV subscriptions and Spotify).

This equated to around $30,000 every year on these three expense items alone.

Obviously, there was more spending on other stuff, but sometimes you can get lost in too much detail.

I then looked at the family's home loan repayments. They were almost equal to what they spent on takeaways, coffee and technology combined. Wow!

Yes, we do need mobile phones in the 21st century, and yes, we do need to enjoy ourselves by eating out, socialising and having fun. But the answer to my client's question was still in the numbers: he and his family were living well beyond their means.

If my clients could rein in their spending, and get back within their monthly budget allowance, then they could destroy their mortgage and pay it off years in advance. That was the original plan!

When they had cleared their debt and saved what they needed to be comfortable, they could then eat all the takeaways they want. This can be their reward for being disciplined and living within their means, focusing on their financial goals and making sure those goals become reality.

When I first started advising, I was always asking clients for a budget. It was a compliance requirement. It was also pointless. Almost every budget completed by the client bore no reflection on their actual spending. They were 'guesstimated'.

To get an accurate picture of their spending, I would ask my clients for their bank statements. If necessary, I would then ask them to reduce their spending to a sustainable level, to make their goals become a reality.

Many would initially reduce their spending; however, very few people possess the true discipline to do so continuously over the long term.

Most people start out with good intentions, but over time they return right back to their bad habits.

The trick is automation: Control and channel your hard-earned money away from you, so that you save it before you spend it.

Set up a system that does this automatically, but be sure to leave you and your family with enough money to have some fun. So how do we do this?

The Pyramid of Control

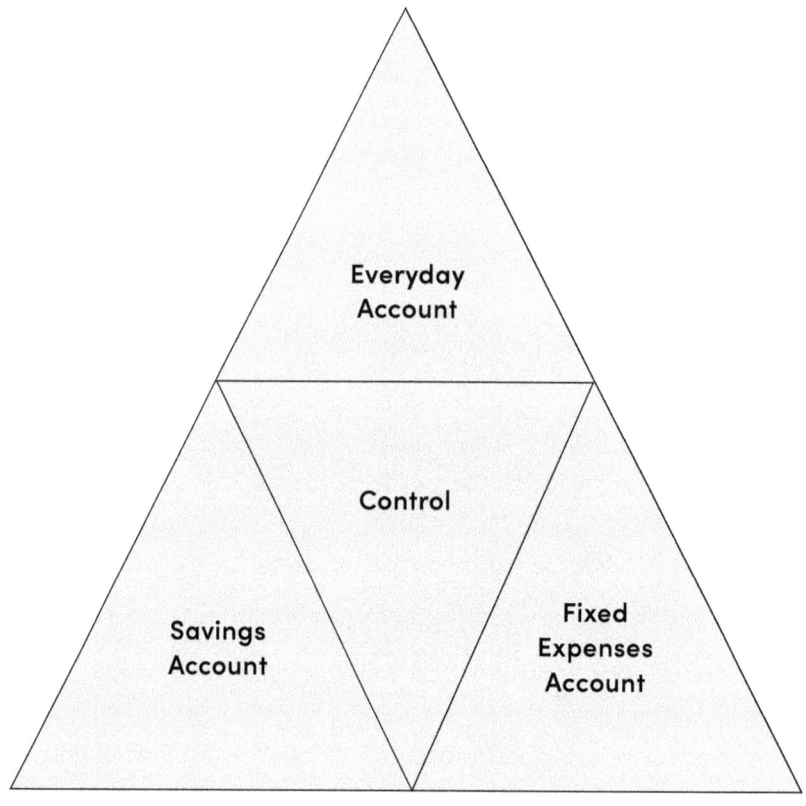

Manage your money with 3 bank accounts, which together form The Pyramid of Control:

1. Everyday Account
2. Fixed Expenses Account
3. Savings Account.

Step 1: Open up your 3 bank accounts

When you create these accounts, literally name them the 'Everyday Account', 'Fixed Expenses Account' and 'Savings Account'.

This separates your money into three parts: two for spending and one for savings. You create a bank account for each part.

This is important because it's how you are going to control the flow of your money toward your order of priorities:

1. Bills and expenses you have to pay.
2. Saving for the future.
3. Spending on things or activities you don't need (but that are fun).

So how do we do this? Firstly, have your income go into your Everyday Account. This is your starting point. (For most people, this will be fortnightly).

Then calculate how much you need to set aside, to pay all of your important bills and 'must pay' expenses.

After that, calculate how much you will save.

Once we have those two amounts, we will set up direct debits for each amount, from your Everyday Account to your Fixed Expenses Account, and to your Savings Account respectively.

We will set up those direct debits for the **very next day** after your regular payday.

Let's calculate those direct debit amounts now.

Step 2: Calculate your fixed expenses and set up a direct debit

Break your spending down into two main areas:

1. Fixed bills and expenses that you must pay. If you don't, you will start to receive nasty letters in the mail; and
2. Discretionary expenses like clothes, eating out, alcohol, gym membership or a trip to a fun park with your family.

By separating your spending into two separate areas, you can prioritise.

Write a list of all your fixed bills and expenses every week, month or quarter. They could include items like:

- home loan repayments
- car loan repayments
- rates
- water
- electricity or gas
- school fees
- internet access
- phones
- house insurance
- car insurance
- health insurance
- pet insurance for your parrot Gertrude (hey, she is family after all).

Next, look at what you spend on groceries in the supermarket. If you want to, set aside an amount for your essentials: meat, bread, milk, vegetables/fruit, baby food, nappies, soap, birdseed, detergent etc. (And no, this does not include takeaway).

If you have an annual family holiday that's very important for you to have, then save for it in your Fixed Expenses Account so you know you will have the funds to pay for it. When saving hard and budgeting, having something to look forward to is motivating.

Don't put the cost of your holiday on a credit card, and create further debt.

The reason why you use your Fixed Expenses Account to save for and pay for your holiday, is that your Savings Account funds should only be used for genuine emergency expenses, and investing in your financial future.

Once you have all your weekly, fortnightly, monthly, quarterly, or irregular fixed bills and expenses, convert each one to an annual figure. Then add them together so you know what the total of your 'absolute must pay' commitments are for a whole year.

Next, divide the figure by 26 so you know how much you need to set aside every fortnight.

Set up a fortnightly direct debit to transfer this amount from your Everyday Account to your Fixed Expenses Account. Arrange for the direct debit to happen the very next day after you get paid each fortnight.

Note: if you get paid monthly, divide your total annual fixed expenses by 12, and arrange a direct debit for this amount to happen the day after you get paid each month.

Let's look at an example spreadsheet.

When creating your spreadsheet, use four column headings:
1. **Bill, expense or repayment** (list each item type).
2. **Amount** (list the cost of each item).
3. **Frequency** (list how often you pay each item).
4. **Annual amount** (list the annual cost of each item).

As you can see in the example, this family has fixed bills, expenses and repayments that amount to $85,294 every year.

To ensure they can pay all their fixed bills throughout the year, they must direct debit $3,281 per fortnight, into their Fixed Expenses Account.

BILL, EXPENSE OR REPAYMENT	AMOUNT	FREQUENCY	ANNUAL AMOUNT
School Fees	$1,500	Quarterly	$6,000
Food	$300	Weekly	$15,600
Council Rates	$1,100	Quarterly	$4,400
Water & Sewerage	$380	Quarterly	$1,520
Car Loan	$720	Monthly	$8,640
Home Loan	$1,230	Fortnightly	$31,980
Gym Membership	$25	Fortnightly	$650
Electricity	$450	Quarterly	$1,800
Gas	$370	Annually	$370
Mobile Phones	$150	Monthly	$1,800
Car Servicing	$750	Annually	$750
Health Insurance	$110	Fortnightly	$2,860
House Insurance	$2,700	Annually	$2,700
Car Insurance	$102	Monthly	$1,224
Family Holiday	$5,000	Annually	$5,000
Total Annual Fixed Costs			$85,294
Total Fixed Costs Fortnightly			$3,281

It would be a good idea to direct debit slightly more than this amount, so if some expenses (such as the electricity bill) are higher, then there will be money in the family's Fixed Expenses Account to pay for them.

Your fixed expense, bill and repayment items will be different to those listed in the example. Use them as a guide and tailor the spreadsheet to reflect all of your fixed expenses, bills and repayments.

Take some time now to create your own spreadsheet, and work out the direct debit amount you need to regularly transfer, from your Everyday Account to your Fixed Expenses Account.

Let's press on, and look at what you need to save, before seeing what is left over to spend on having fun.

Summary for Winning Number 3
Create 3 accounts to manage the flow of money:
1. An account to pay your fixed commitments with.
2. An account to save with.
3. An account to have fun with.

Create your Pyramid of Control!

Winning Number 20: Saving

> *"Do not save what is left after spending, but spend what is left after saving."*
> — Warren Buffett

Step 3: Save

Work out what 20% of your after-tax salary is.

Set up a direct debit to transfer this amount from your Everyday Account to your Savings Account the day after your regular payday.

Why 20%? This amount is what you should be aiming to save as a minimum, because 20% is enough to have a material impact on your financial life.

If you can save more, great! But don't be unrealistic with your savings goal — it needs to be sustainable and achievable.

So, what will these savings be used for?

They will be used to build an emergency fund, clear bad debt, and invest in your (and your family's) future.

Every dollar that you save in this account should only go toward items that genuinely progress you financially.

And no, a 75-inch TV with surround sound is not on that list!

Your Savings Account is there firstly for emergencies.

So how much should you save for your emergency fund?

The amount will vary from person to person and family to family. As a rule of thumb, you should aim to save enough to cover at least four months of your expenses, as an absolute minimum.

You should then continue to build up this amount to at least six months of your total living expenses, and maintain this amount in your Savings Account. When you do, it will give you the peace of mind that you can deal with life's curve balls.

To confirm: having four months of living expenses in your Savings Account, is what I consider to be the line in the sand when it comes to emergency savings. Having over six months of your living expenses in savings, is what I consider to be the 'comfort zone'.

The initial four-month minimum will make more sense after you read about personal insurance later in this book.

Once you have at least 6 months' worth of living expenses saved, you can start to look at investing some of those 'excess' savings to build your wealth.

If you have a mortgage and an offset account, then use your offset account as your savings account. (I talk more about offset accounts later in the book).

Ultimately, you should never stop building your savings: you will have emergencies that will deplete these funds from time to time, and life always gets more expensive.

Step 4: Spend and have fun!

What you have left in your Everyday Account (after your direct debits to your Fixed Expense Account and your Savings Account) is what you can spend to have fun with, and spoil yourself.

Be careful with your spending from your Everyday Account. Once it's empty, there are no more beers at the pub, until the next time you get paid.

Note to self: the Everyday Account is where you pay your Netflix and Spotify direct debits. They are not essential bills: they are luxuries. Just because they are fixed commitments does not mean they come out of your Fixed Expense Account!

If you can, have any direct debits from your Everyday Account for fun stuff, set up for the day after you get paid. This ensures there will be funds to cover them. We all know there is nothing like a Netflix binge in winter ☺.

The Winning Numbers 3 and 20 in action

Let's run through a simple breakdown of how a two-income family is using the Winning Numbers 3 and 20 to take care of their fixed bills, save and have fun at the same time on an after-tax income of $5,750 per fortnight.

Step 1	Open three accounts. Pay goes into Everyday Account	$5,750
Step 2	Fixed Expenses Account — direct debit from Everyday Account	$3,300
Step 3	Savings Account — direct debit (20% of $5,750) from Everyday Account	$1,150
Step 4	Amount left over in Everyday Account — to spend on whatever you want	$1,300

THE SEVEN WINNING NUMBERS

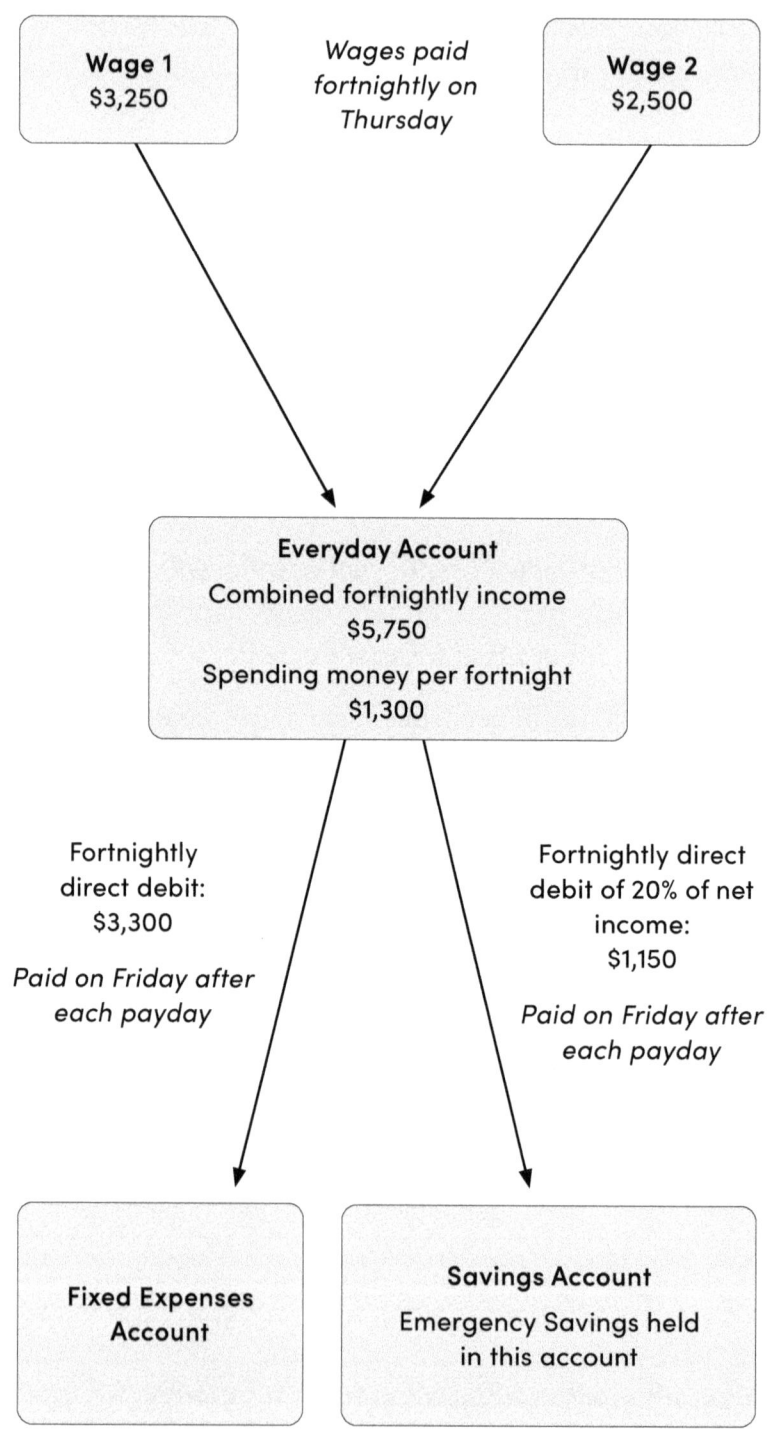

In this scenario, the whole family is allowed to spend $1,300 per fortnight on whatever they want — football tickets, beers at the pub, eating out, sports clothes, movie tickets or anything else — without needing to worry about money.

They can enjoy this money and have fun, because while they are, they will also be saving $1,150 every fortnight.

If you multiply $1,150 by 26 times in a year, you will see that this family will save $29,900 in just 12 months!

Question: If you apply The Winning Numbers of 3 and 20 to your life, who is in control of your money?

Answer: You are!

You will be living within your means, making sure your bills are paid, saving, and still be able to have fun.

And what will you have really achieved by setting up three bank accounts and saving 20% of your income?

You will have created the foundation of your financial success!

Just by having the three bank account strategy, you will be ahead of most of the people you know. Why? Because you are in control of your money, and they are not.

And who are most people?

Your work colleagues, family members and friends.
People you already know.

If something bad happens and they need money, most people put it on their credit card. Or they ring their bank in a panic asking for an increase on their home loan.

Most people don't have savings set aside.

The very existence of companies like Afterpay is living proof of how many people live beyond their means. They actually live from pay packet to pay packet.

If you are one of them, there are multi-millionaires who own these companies making a fortune off you, because you are letting them.

They are getting richer, and you are getting nowhere. But not for much longer!

So many people end up poor simply because they do not save. But not you!

 Summary for Winning Number 20
Save 20% of your after-tax salary to clear bad debt, build up an emergency fund, and invest in your (and your family's) future.

Now, let's clarify something important! What are we doing with the 20% of our wage that we are saving?

1. **Clearing any bad debt you have.**

   Bad debt is any debt you owe from buying something that holds no value, or goes down in value (for example, a holiday paid on a credit card, a car or furniture bought on finance).

   Bad debt does nothing to advance you financially. It only makes you go backwards.

   However, bad debt does not include your home loan. Your home loan (or mortgage) allows you to put a roof over your head. And your home, whilst not paying you an income, has the potential to go up in value. It is a good debt.

   Good debt is any debt that is used to buy an asset that goes up in value, and/or pays you income in the form of a dividend, rent or interest. Good debt, when used wisely, has the ability to help you create wealth, and strengthen your financial position.

   Bad debt always weakens your financial position. Always.

   I'll explain how you can clear any bad debt that you have, in the next section of this chapter.

2. **Building up your emergency savings.**

   This will help you to deal with any financial emergency that comes your way. The amount you need will depend on your personal circumstances, and personal preferences.

   Remember the rule of thumb: save and maintain four to six months' worth of your current expenses — at a minimum.

   Ideally this emergency fund will continue to grow, giving you even more financial security in case of emergencies.

3. **Investing surplus funds once you have your emergency savings in place.**

   It's important to build up your investments outside of super, to help you reach your financial goals and achieve financial security.

   How much should you invest? Well, that depends on how much you save.

   For example, if you direct debit 20% of your wage into your Savings Account, then you could set up a regular investing strategy where you invest three-quarters of those savings.

   You could then leave the other quarter in your Savings Account to build your savings balance further. Let's apply this strategy using the figures in the earlier example.

   - Assume you are saving $1,150 per fortnight.
   - You could invest three-quarters or 75% ($862.50) of that amount into a managed investment fund. Or if it makes it easier, round the amount to $860.
   - You could retain one-quarter or 25% ($287.50) in your savings account to grow your emergency savings further. Or if it makes it easier, round the amount to $290.

   You are taking money out of your Savings Account and investing it, but also continuing to grow your emergency savings above the minimum recommended amount.

   We will talk a lot more about investing in Part 2 of this book.

Debt — Take Control of Your Debt and Stop it Controlling You!

> *"Too many people spend money they haven't earned, to buy things they don't want, to impress people that they don't like".*
>
> — *Will Rogers (performer and social commentator)*

Before we can embark on a journey of saving and investing for the future, we need to get control of our debt and make it disappear.

There is no point saving and investing if you're paying 10% to 20% interest on a loan.

You are much better off to pay this expensive, blood-sucking debt off first.

It can be easy to get into trouble with debt. And sometimes you don't realise you are in trouble, until it's too late.

Largely gone are the days when if you saw something you wanted in a department store, you either paid for the item in full, or you saved up for it. If you didn't have the funds saved, and you didn't want anyone else purchasing the item, you would put the item on 'lay-by' with the store lay-by department. You would pay a deposit, and then make further deposits on it every payday, until you've saved up and paid in full. Only then did the store allow you to take your new prized possession home!

My mum used to do this when I was a kid, and the idea seems so strange now. But what was lay-by really? It was a forced type of saving. No debt or interest was ever involved.

In the days before Afterpay, AMEX, Diners Club, fuel cards, store cards, in-store finance and overdrafts, lay-by was the only option you had if you couldn't afford to pay for something.

But now:

Who needs to lay-by?

Who needs to save?

Just borrow and have what you want now instead, and embrace the era of instant gratification!

If you are struggling with debt and feel like you're drowning, then let's look at how to take control.

How do we smash your debt down as fast as possible?

List all of your loans on a spreadsheet with four columns that have the following headings:

1. **Debt type** (what the loan is for)
2. **Amount owing**
3. **Interest rate**
4. **Monthly repayment.**

Normally you would prioritise the debt with the highest interest rate. After all, it's costing you the most interest, right?

No, what we want to do here is free up your cash flow by clearing smaller debts first. *Crossing a debt off the list will also give you a motivational boost to keep going!*

Once those smaller debts are gone and more of your cash is freed up, we use that additional cash to speed up the destruction of the bigger debts, until all of them have been obliterated.

Let's look at an example of a person who has gone for the 'buy now, pay later' approach to life.

DEBT TYPE	AMOUNT OWING	INTEREST RATE	MONTHLY REPAYMENT
Secured Car Loan	$27,000	8%	$720
In-Store Loan (Furniture)	$14,000	5.5%	$297
Unsecured Personal Loan	$3,500	13%	$185
Credit Card	$7,000	20%	$231
TOTAL AMOUNT OWING	$51,500		$1,433

The loan term is not as important here. When we are finished, you will be paying off your loans before their terms are up!

As you can see in this scenario, this person has acquired a decent amount of personal debt. With repayments costing $1,433 every month; they are struggling.

They cannot save and therefore cannot get ahead!

If you are in a position like this, how should you approach your debt to pay it down as fast as possible?

Your debt should be prioritised in this order:

1. unsecured personal loan
2. credit card
3. in-store loan (furniture)
4. secured car loan.

Again, we are not initially targeting the debt with the highest interest rate in this case: the credit card.

We are going to go after the unsecured personal loan first, because it is the smallest debt and will be quickest to pay off.

Use the 20% of your income that you allocate to savings, to pay out the unsecured personal loan first.

By doing so, you will free up $185 per month in repayments, that you can add to your credit card repayments — which is the second debt-elimination target on your priority list.

You will then use your 20% savings plus the freed up $185 per month (your former repayment for the now paid-off unsecured personal loan) to pay your credit card debt off.

When you do, you will free up another $231 per month.

You will then use your 20% savings once again, plus the freed up $185 and $231 per month, to target your furniture loan.

By adding all of these amounts to the $297 per month that you are already paying for your furniture, you will clear the amount you owe in no time.

Once your personal loan, credit card and furniture loan are gone, you will have freed up $713 per month to put toward your car loan. Its days are numbered!

> **What are the key points for clearing debt?**
> - Target one loan at a time.
> - Free up your cash flow, and add the freed up amount to the next loan to pay it off even faster.
> - This is commonly called 'the domino effect'.
> - It is the go-to strategy for all licensed financial advisers when helping clients to clear debt.

Car loans

Most of us need a car to get to work, take the kids to school, buy groceries and get around. And most of us have to borrow money to buy a car, because we have not saved enough to buy one outright.

If that's you, make it your mission to pay off your car loan as quickly as possible.

Borrowing money to buy a car is bad debt, because from the day you buy that car to the day you sell it, it loses value.

You are paying interest just to own a depreciating asset.

The risk with buying a car funded by finance, is that one day the car could be worth less than what you owe.

Worse, you may need to replace the car if it's become too expensive to repair, while you still owe money on it!

I've seen it happen where people buy a new car on finance, and sell the old car, but can't clear the old loan from the sale of the old car. The outcome is one car, and two debts.

So, what is the rule of thumb here?

If you ever borrow money to buy a car:
1. borrow on a term of no more than 5 years
2. never have a balloon payment (a large final repayment) if leasing a car
3. be ambitious and set a goal to pay your car off in less than 5 years.

This will help prevent the situation where you owe more than the car is worth.

But there are other reasons to pay a car loan off faster.

When it comes to how much interest you pay on a loan, there's not only the interest rate to consider, it's also the time you take to pay off the loan.

Interest paid = Loan Term x Loan Amount x Interest Rate.

Let's look at an example.

TERM OF LOAN	AMOUNT BORROWED	INTEREST RATE	TOTAL INTEREST PAID
7 years	$45,000	8%	$13,916
5 years	$45,000	10%	$12,367

In this scenario we can see that the interest rate for the five-year loan is higher than the seven-year loan, but because the seven-year loan has a longer time frame, more interest is payable overall.

I frequently see seven-year terms for car loans, because people just want lower regular repayment amounts — and think nothing more of it.

The longer you owe money for, the more interest you pay.

Reducing the amount you borrow, may mean that you have to buy the base model of a car. Or even buy a totally different car to the one you really want in order to reduce the loan amount. By doing this, however, you will reduce your repayments to an amount you can afford.

If that's what you have to do to ensure the term of the loan is no more than five years, then that's what you have to do. The sacrifice you make, will be worth it.

Why? Because you are taking control of your financial future, and living within your means.

This is you ensuring those financial dreams that you wrote down before, actually become a reality!

You're in charge, not the salesman in the car yard!

Credit cards — should I have one?

If there is a usual suspect when it comes to drowning in debt, it is the credit card.

If you have ever ended up in trouble with debt, then you probably think credit cards are Satan's preferred form of finance. They kind of are.

If you can't clear the balance of your credit card before the interest-free period ends, then you have a credit card limit that is too high, or you are spending too much money each month.

I just don't see rewards points as being sufficient reason to pay for things using a credit card. Some people love them, and pay for as much as they possibly can with one. They collect the points in the hope that one day they can go on a holiday with a free flight.

I see how much trouble people can get themselves into financially with a credit card, and as a result, I remain wary of them regardless of other peoples' love of them.

Credit cards and fraud

One argument that I believe is plausible when it comes to having a credit card, is protection against fraud when buying stuff online. Credit cards have 100% protection against fraud: if your card is used fraudulently, you don't pay the amount stolen. Plus, it is someone else's money the fraudsters have stolen, so what do you care? Just report the fraud and move on.

With a debit card, it's not so clear-cut. There is some protection against fraud with a debit card, but not as much as there is for a credit card. (It depends on the card provider).

If someone uses your debit card fraudulently, they have spent *your* money. And it is no longer in *your* bank account. You need to get it back. You will be without those funds, until the bank or card provider completes its investigation of the fraud.

See the difference? Credit cards come with 100% fraud protection, and it's not your money that was stolen.

However, sometimes keeping things simple is best. If you do not need a credit card, do not have one. Keep the temptation to overspend out of your life.

I know some people will disagree with my opinion on credit cards. If you do decide you need to have a credit card, ensure that your credit limit and use allows you to clear the balance in full every month. Never pay interest on this type of lending.

When it comes to building wealth and credit cards:

- You should never pay 20% interest (or whatever extortionate rate the bank is charging you for credit card debt) especially when you've probably used the card to buy something that you don't need.
- There is nothing so important that you need to pay 20% interest in order to have it. You will never get ahead financially if you do.

Defaulting on debt

If you know you will not be able to make a loan repayment or credit card payment on time, do not throw your hands into the air and admit defeat. It is important to keep going and not give up.

When it comes to consumer debt, lenders have to comply with consumer credit law.

There are several things you can do during this stressful time, which will greatly benefit you:

- **Contact your lender immediately.**

    Tell them before you miss a repayment if you know that you will. Otherwise, contact them as soon as possible about the payment you have missed.

    Be open about your situation. Communicate — preferably by email or another written method — so everything is documented. Explain that you wish to keep making your repayments, but that you are currently not able to. Your lender will explain the options available to you.

- **Keep making a part-payment, even if it is a small amount.**

    Do not stop paying, if you can. There is a difference between being behind on repayments, and completely defaulting on debt.

    By continuing to make part-repayments you are showing a commitment and willingness to try to repay your debts. Your part-repayments will also reduce the penalty interest the lender charges you.

- **Negotiate and discuss creating a new repayment plan with your lender.**

If you agree to a new repayment plan with your lender before you miss a repayment, then the impact on your credit score is significantly less than if you wait until you have completely missed repayments.

Once you have agreed to a new repayment plan — stick to it. Your lender should guide you through the new payment plan, and allow you sufficient time to get back on track financially.

While a bank or other lender may seem to be a giant 'beast' with no feelings, the people you are dealing with in the credit department are humans, and can be reasoned with. They will appreciate your openness and honesty, and they will respect your efforts if you continue to make loan repayments to get back on track.

- **Don't just assume if you default on a payment, that is the end.**

    Never stop communicating, and never just stop paying. Because that is when the debt collectors start knocking on your door, and your credit score takes a dive.

- **There are professional debt management organisations out there that can take over negotiations and the management of your money and debt.**

    They will contact your lenders, correspond with them, and establish debt management plans on your behalf. But be aware that this will come at a cost to you, on top of paying back any debt. There is no free lunch.

- **If you do feel overwhelmed, call the government funded National Debt Helpline on 1800 007 007 to speak to a financial counsellor.**

    They are there to help. We have all been there — don't give up!

Winning Number 55: The 'Danger Zone'

Early in my career I had a lovely couple walk into the office for their first appointment. Well, they didn't really walk in. The lady walked holding the arm of her husband as he hobbled in obvious discomfort. Without his wife's physical support, he wouldn't have made it through the door.

When they finally sat down, I asked them to tell me their story.

They were both 62 years of age. He was a carpenter, and she worked in administration. He needed both knees replaced and was worn out physically.

He had been to Centrelink (the Department of Social Security) to try and get the Disability Support Pension. He was too young for the Age Pension, which at the time didn't start until age 65 (and now starts at age 67).

Centrelink had declined his application for the Disability Support Pension. Why? Because he was broken physically, but (in their eyes at least) not disabled: he just got old, early.

Centrelink gave him a partial Job Seeker Allowance, even though he struggled to walk — let alone work.

The problem was, the partial Job Seeker Allowance he received was not enough to pay the couple's home loan repayments plus all their other bills, even when combined with his wife's wage.

Given that he was in constant physical pain and couldn't walk properly, it was unlikely he would ever work again.

This lovely couple had spent four years renovating their home, and planned for it to be their 'home in retirement'. They had funded the renovations by drawing from their home loan, and still owed $450,000.

I couldn't believe how much they owed at their age.

I looked at their financial situation from every angle, but I knew they had to sell the house to clear their mortgage. They were gutted.

They sold their house and downsized into an apartment, which neither of them wanted to do. It felt like a prison cell for the husband.

As for their pet dog? No dogs were allowed in the apartment complex, so they had to give their beloved black labrador away. As a dog lover, I would be truly gutted at that prospect.

So, what is the key message here?

Debt is a legal obligation to pay back money by a certain date, regardless of whether you are able to or not.

Debt allowed this couple to firstly buy their home and then to renovate it. The thing is, at some stage you have to pay debt back, and after a change in their circumstances — they couldn't.

They realised (belatedly) what debt really is.

Debt is like a fire: it's a great servant, but a horrible master.

As we get older, the chances of us getting injured or sick increases. In many industries, our employability decreases with age. We don't like the thought of being put out to pasture, but we live in a competitive world.

Getting back into the workforce becomes harder as we get older should injury, illness, or unemployment strike.

This couple were now in what I call the 'Danger Zone'.

I'm not talking about being a fighter pilot who 'feels the need for speed' and the desire to break the sound barrier.

This 'Danger Zone' is between the ages of 55 and 65.

I have met so many small-business owners who are tired when they reach 55. They don't necessarily want to stop working, but they want to reduce their hours, and be relieved of the stress of running a business.

I have also met school teachers, tradesmen and delivery truck drivers who are realising in their mid-fifties that the fire in their bellies that created their passion for their work, is going out. They either want to retire fully, or semi-retire and work part-time.

If you have ever been made redundant, you might have experienced the initial euphoria of a couple of weeks off. You may also admire your redundancy payout for a while. But eventually, you will have to decide to go back to work because you realise that despite the redundancy payment, you cannot afford to retire.

You are now in direct competition with other prospective employees.

Imagine this scenario: one day you are sitting in an office reception room, nervously waiting for a job interview. While you are rubbing your sweaty palms on your seat, you notice a 35-year-old prospect coming out of the interview room, brimming with positivity and youthful (yet measured) energy. The 35-year-old is well qualified, has 10 years under their belt, and plenty of ambition. You are 55 and only want to put another five years in.

If you were an employer, who would you choose?

Crying out "Ageism is a form of discrimination" will not help you. Remember, we are dealing with reality, not the idealistic world we want it to be. Competitive pressure will often force an employer's hand.

If you are a tradie or do a physical job, your body will tell you one day it can't do what it used to. You will either have to stop working, or retrain for another job in your late 50s.

Call centre work anyone?

Sorry if I offended anyone in a call centre. You do a great job by the way!

If there is one thing I have learnt over the years, it is that you need to pay your home loan off faster than the bank wants.

And if you do a physical job, you need to pay your mortgage off well before your body calls it a day.

Unfortunately, many people who have a mortgage on their home will simply not pay it off before they retire — and yet they do nothing about it.

They start dreaming about retirement well before they can conceivably pay their mortgage off, but have no plan in place to actually make that happen.

Some couples I've met talk about downsizing as a way of clearing their mortgage. My first response is, "Have you looked at other places to live?"

"No."

"I recommend that you do."

I make a suggestion that they look at the suburbs where they want to downsize and retire to (quite often they are near the beach) and then look at the price of the homes in that area.

When I see them again, they have often realised that the only places they are happy with, have similar prices to their existing home.

Downsizing doesn't necessarily result in down valuing: it doesn't guarantee that you will release sufficient equity to pay off your debt.

By the time you've paid real estate agent fees and stamp duty, you've gone backwards. And if you throw 'clearing the home loan' into the equation, you may not have enough left to buy another decent house to live in!

I'm not saying that downsizing doesn't work. You just need to do your homework. I've had clients successfully downsize, become debt-free, and live quite happily in their new abode.

I have also had clients release equity from their home through downsizing. They then invest these funds in super and supplement their Age Pension, boosting the income that they have to fund their retirement.

The age of 55 is also the age when personal insurance premiums start to become very expensive. This is no coincidence.

Personal insurance premiums are priced according to statistics. Age 55 and above is when people start to claim on their personal insurance a lot more often.

Do not enter the Danger Zone with a mortgage.

Set a goal to pay your home loan off fully, by the age of 55.

So, what will you achieve by paying your home loan off by age 55? You will remove the biggest financial burden you have.

If you become injured, ill or redundant, you won't have to worry about where the money comes from to pay the bank back.

And if you just want to reduce the hours you work and take your foot off the pedal of life, you can.

Summary for Winning Number 55
Stay away from the 'Danger Zone'!

Pay your home loan off by age 55. How? With the winning number 4.

"SLOW DOWN, CYRIL!
JUST BECAUSE WE AVOIDED ONE DANGER ZONE,
DOESN'T MEAN WE SHOULD ENTER ANOTHER ONE!"

Winning Number 4: Paying your mortgage off faster

So how do you pay your home loan off faster, and by the age of 55?

There are 4 strategies you can use:

1. **Pay fortnightly.**
2. **Make extra fortnightly repayments.**
3. **Have an offset account attached.**
4. **Refinance to a lower interest rate.**

Let's take a look at these strategies in a bit more detail:

Strategy 1: Paying fortnightly

I am surprised when I meet people who get paid fortnightly but who actually pay their home loan repayments monthly.

Why is this an issue?

Well, interest is calculated daily on a home loan, and charged monthly to your loan balance.

So, if you pay fortnightly, for about half of that month you owe just a little bit less.

Then the interest that accrues daily on your home loan balance is also just a little bit less for that month.

If you multiply this small interest saving by 26 fortnights a year, and then multiply this amount by your loan term (usually 20 to 30 years), you have a mathematical outcome that Albert Einstein would be proud of!

By paying fortnightly instead of monthly you can take several years off a home loan, saving you thousands of dollars

in interest when you haven't paid a single dollar more in repayments. You've just paid more frequently!

Note: Even if you get paid monthly, you can still pay your home loan fortnightly!

Strategy 2: Making extra repayments

Your scheduled home loan repayments go toward paying the interest on your home loan, and a certain amount off the principal that you owe the bank.

In the early years, most of what you make in repayments goes toward the interest on your home loan.

But when it comes to making extra repayments, the entire 'extra' amount goes to reducing your outstanding loan balance.

None of this extra loan repayment is consumed by interest.

With those extra home loan repayments, you are chipping away faster at your outstanding balance.

If you can make those extra repayments each fortnight, it's even better. Multiply those extra 26 repayment amounts by the term of your home loan and it's even more mathematical magic.

Strategy 3: An offset account

An offset account is just a transactional or savings account that has been linked to your home loan. They are great. If your home loan has a variable interest rate, you should be able to have an offset account attached.

Here is how an offset account works: For every dollar held in your offset account, the bank pretends you owe a dollar less on your linked home loan.

For example, if you have:

A home loan balance of...	$500,000
An offset account balance of...	$50,000
You are only charged interest on...	$450,000

By being charged less interest on your home loan, more of your standard home loan repayments go toward paying off the actual debt.

And, if you think about it, you will be effectively earning tax-free interest on your savings at the same interest rate as your home loan (which is higher than standard deposit rates).

Not only that, you can access the funds any time. How good is that!

If you already have a home loan and an offset account, the 20% of your net income you are saving via direct debit should be going straight into your offset account.

If your bank won't attach an offset account to your home loan, either change the type of home loan you have, or change banks.

With interest rates rising, offset accounts will be even more effective in getting your mortgage down faster. For some borrowers, interest rates (as at March 2023) are now approaching — or are higher — than 6% on home loans.

Tell me now where you can get a risk-free and tax-free 6% return — or more — on your investment? I can tell you where: Nowhere!

Strategy 4: Refinancing your home loan

One of the reasons why banks and mortgage brokers love locking you into a fixed interest rate on your home loan, is because they have locked you in as a customer. To refinance out of a fixed rate home loan to another bank comes with a breaking fee — and those fees can be expensive. The cost depends on the time left on the fixed rate period, and the interest rate. The longer you have left, the higher the fee.

If you have a variable rate home loan, you can refinance with another bank anytime and not incur this break fee.

When it comes to a bank, loyalty does not pay!

A bank has a relationship with your money, not you. They will never ring you up and say:

> *"Dear Mrs. Smith, because you have been a very loyal customer of the bank for 20 years, we are reducing your interest rate on your home loan by 0.5%, just for being a good egg."*

It doesn't happen.

Banks offer their best introductory rate to new customers, and hope that once you are on board, you become lazy and can't be bothered moving to another bank.

And you know what, most people *are* lazy. So, it works!

Who wants the fuss of signing application forms, finding your pay slips, doing a budget, finding old bank statements, and getting a letter from your employer to prove you have a job?

And then you have to move all of your direct debits to a new account!

At the end of the day: this is a first world problem.

Ring your bank. Ask if they can better the interest rate you are currently being charged. If they can't, then engage the services of a mortgage broker. See if they can better your existing home loan. Let them do the heavy lifting.

If they can reduce your existing home loan rate by a decent margin, then great. If not, it has cost you nothing.

> When comparing loan interest rates: look at both the interest rate and the comparison rate. What is the comparison rate?
>
> The comparison rate is where the bank adds all their fees and charges into the cost of the finance, and converts it all to an equivalent interest rate, to make it easier for you to compare overall cost.
>
> With all the various bank fees and charges, comparing home loans can be difficult.
>
> With a comparison rate these fees and charges have been taken into account, all you need to compare is the interest rate. Now, you can compare apples with apples, instead of apples with bananas, oranges or lemons.
>
> The comparison rate is a better guide on the true cost of finance.
>
> The lower the comparison rate, the better.

Using a mortgage calculator

There is a great online home loan calculator called AMP Rapid Pay.[3] I find it easier to use than the ASIC Moneysmart Mortgage Calculator, which is an alternative to consider. Look for the calculator using an internet search engine and bring it up on your computer screen.

Let's run through four home loan scenarios using the AMP Rapid Pay online calculator:

THE SEVEN WINNING NUMBERS

Scenario 1	Paying monthly as the default option
Scenario 2	Refinancing from a 4.5% loan interest rate down to 4.25%
Scenario 3	Scenario 2 plus paying fortnightly instead of monthly
Scenario 4	Scenario 2 and 3 plus making extra repayments of $250 per fortnight

Note: these interest rates are for illustration purposes and may not be current market rates offered by lenders.

Key home loan information:

- Home loan amount: $500,000
- Loan term: 30 years
- Interest rate 4.5%.

SCENARIO	LOAN AMOUNT	ORIGINAL LOAN TERM: (YEARS)	NEW LOAN TERM: (YEARS AND MONTHS)	ORIGINAL INTEREST COST	NEW INTEREST COST	INTEREST SAVED
1	$500,000	30	30y	$412,032	$412,032	$0
2	$500,000	30	30y	$412,032	$385,491	$26,541
3	$500,000	30	25y9m	$412,032	$320,649	$91,383
4	$500,000	30	19y	$412,032	$227,170	$184,862

With every step you take, you reduce the amount of interest you pay. When you combine all steps together, you make a significant impact on your home loan term. You can see in this example that by doing the following:

- Refinancing your loan and saving ¼ of a percent
- Plus making fortnightly repayments instead of monthly,
- Plus making additional repayments of $250 per fortnight.

You can get a 30-year half-a-million dollar home loan paid off in 19 years, and save yourself $184,862 in interest.

Now that's an impressive result!

Note: In the above example, I have not included a scenario with an offset account. Your plan may be that you invest some or most of your savings and just leave the emergency savings in your offset account. If I did include an offset account in the scenario, the result would be even better.

Why don't you put all of your own existing loan details into the AMP Rapid Pay online tool, and then apply one or more of the four early repayment strategies:

- Change to fortnightly repayments instead of monthly.
- Make extra loan repayments.
- Add an offset account.
- Reduce your interest rate to a lower rate that's available in the market.

Look at the difference these strategies make!

> **Summary for Winning Number 4**
>
> Apply the online home loan calculator to your situation. What do you need to do to repay your home loan by age 55? How much do you need to repay per fortnight in order to clear your home loan by age 55? Can you make this happen? Make it happen! Apply The Winning Number 4.

Winning Number 10: Finding another 10% savings

> *"Frugality includes all the other virtues."*
> — Cicero (Roman statesman)

You didn't think I would let you get away with it did you?

So far, you have automated your savings and spending to ensure all your fixed bills are covered. You are also setting aside 20% of your pay packet to save, attack any bad debts, build up an emergency fund and invest.

Now it's time to look at each and every bill to identify what you spend your money on, and see if you can save a little bit more.

So, what are we looking for here?

An extra 10% of savings off what you spend.

Yes, that's right, 10 is the second Winning Number that will help you pay your home loan off faster.

I want you to find an extra 10% of savings from your fixed bills and 'having fun' spending.

How are you going to do that you ask?

Well let me tell you a story about how to play the system.

Every year I would receive a letter from our house and contents insurer. They would automatically renew our insurance 'for our convenience'. And in doing so, continue to provide us with valuable cover to protect our most important financial asset: our home.

They would emphasise we did not need to do anything; our insurance would just continue. What great guys!

What they also did was increase the premium by an extortionate amount that was way above the inflation rate every year.

Finally, last year, I'd had enough.

Frustrated with the continued increases, I rang the insurer and asked them if they could do anything about reducing the cost of insurance.

Their response: "No Sir, we don't offer any discounts off the premium."

I then asked them to quote me the same home and contents cover with the 'specified items' and 'portable items' removed.

They came back with 10% off the current premium: just a few hundred dollars.

This wasn't enough — and I was still cross. So, I went onto their online quoting tool and completed a quote for my house for the exact amount of cover I already had on my home and general contents, but without the portable or specified items.

I remembered originally doing the online quote for our house and contents insurance a few years ago, and noted the big difference the 'specified items' and 'portable items' made to the cost of our cover.

The new quote was $1,900 cheaper!

I then thought about the fact that our home borders onto a forest reserve, and is in a high fire danger zone. I also thought about the increased cost of building materials and increased labour costs as a result of COVID-induced inflation. So, I increased the home cover amount for the building itself.

The overall new premium was still $1,600 less than I was currently paying, even though I insured the building for more.

And all of this was with the same insurer.

No, I'm not kidding!

I decided to cancel my existing cover by a certain date.

I applied for and got new cover **with the same insurer**, making sure the start of the new cover was the same day the old policy stopped, and saved myself $1,600 per annum.

My wife and I decided to not take the premium increases lying down. We also decided to prioritise insuring what was vital, and not insure what we could survive without.

I have kept my old home and contents policy statements to remind me of this lesson.

Review all of your bills and fixed expenses annually. Shop around. Look for better deals.

You can also look hard at what luxuries you do and don't need. For example, maybe just one pay TV provider is all you really need, not two or three.

So, what are you going to do with that extra 10% you save off expenses?

You are going to allocate it to your home loan as your 'extra' fortnightly repayments.

Once you have found those 10% savings off your expenses, you then set up another direct debit from your Fixed Expenses Account for that 10% to go directly to your home loan.

Make those repayments fortnightly, so divide your additional 10% in annual savings by 26.

To clarify: your extra fortnightly home loan repayment does not go into your offset account as savings, it goes directly to your home loan instead to reduce the outstanding balance you owe the bank.

Spend some time now and revisit the AMP Rapid Pay online calculator.[4] *Add the additional repayments to the equation along with your lower interest rate, normal fortnightly repayments and offset account balance.*

Does this get you debt-free by age 55? If so, great!

If not, try to find even more savings from your spending.

Summary for Winning Number 10
Find an extra 10% to save from your spending. Use the 10% you save as extra fortnightly home loan repayments. **Avoid the 'Danger Zone'.**

Winning Number 5: An extra 5% a day keeps the doctor away

When it comes to saving for retirement in Australia, superannuation is your best friend. Nothing beats it!

When you use superannuation as a vehicle for saving for your retirement, you save on tax in two ways:

1. Concessional (before tax) contributions to super are taxed at a maximum rate of just 15%[5]. This is a lot less than most people's marginal tax rates (see the table below).[6]
2. The profits made by you inside superannuation are also taxed at a maximum rate of only 15%. Most super funds pay even less than 15% tax after claiming tax deductions, tax refunds and capital gains tax discounts.

TAXABLE INCOME	MARGINAL TAX RATE*	TAX ON THIS INCOME
0 TO $18,200	0%	Nil
$18,201 TO $45,000	19%	19 cents for each $1 over $18,200
$45,001 TO $120,000	32.5%	$5,092 plus 32.5 cents for each $1 over $45,000
$120,001 TO $180,000	37%	$29,467 plus 37 cents for each $1 over $120,000
$180,001 AND OVER	45%	$51,667 plus 45 cents for each $1 over $180,000

*The above rates do not include the Medicare levy of 2%.

Thus, investing via super not only reduces the income tax you pay, it also makes investing for retirement a lot more tax-efficient.

Once you retire, and are 60 years of age or over, you can gain access to your super savings and use these savings to fund your retirement. One option is to roll your super fund into an Account Based Pension. Once this happens, you can pay yourself a totally tax-free pension, plus any profits made inside your super fund whilst in the pension phase are also totally tax-free.

Not only is saving for retirement via superannuation tax-efficient, it also locks away your retirement savings until at least the age of 60 (or the 'preservation age'). This means you can't access these funds until then. This is a good thing because everyone has a bad day.

Can you imagine if every time you went through a rough patch, and wanted to cheer yourself up with some retail therapy or a holiday, you could get access to your super? There would be nothing left!

Look at what happened during COVID when the federal government let anyone who wanted to, get hold of up to $20,000 from their super.[7] There was just no need to do this and most of it was spent on stuff people didn't need.

There are thousands of people in Australia who every evening stare at their 75-inch, ultra-high definition television that was bought with early release super funds.

"HONEY, IS THERE ANYTHING GOOD TO WATCH TONIGHT ON THE SUPER FUND?"

$20,000 taken out of super now is $20,000 that does not build and grow for retirement. It is worth much more to you in 20 years' time: even at a conservative rate of return of 5%, it will be worth $53,066.

But there are other benefits of investing via a superannuation fund. Did you know that creditors (for example, your bank) and litigants (people who sue you) cannot touch your super? Your super is protected from them because your super funds are held in trust.

The only way a creditor or litigant can get access to your super, is by proving in court that you hid your money in super solely so you didn't have to pay back your debts. But for the vast majority of us, this will not apply.

Your employer has to contribute 10.5% of your salary into your super fund by law, and this amount will progressively increase to 12% by 1 July 2025.[8] You can voluntarily contribute more than this amount: up to a total combined amount of $27,500 per annum, concessionally taxed at only 15%[9].

It's important that you don't contribute more than this amount though because if you do, any excess amount will be taxed at your higher marginal tax rate.

A good way to voluntarily save into super is to 'salary sacrifice'. This means asking your payroll officer at work to take more out of your pay before it's taxed, and contribute it into your super fund.

If you're on a salary of $95,000 per annum, your marginal tax rate including the Medicare levy is 34.5%.

This means that for every $1 you salary sacrifice into your super, you save 19.5 cents in tax. Nice!

That's effectively a risk-free 19.5% return on your investment — and you haven't invested it yet.

Where do I sign up?

Let's run through an example of what happens to your super if you contribute an additional 5% of your salary, and you're on a salary of $95,000 per annum.

The table on the following page shows that by contributing an additional 5% of your pre-tax income (i.e., $4,750 per year) via salary sacrifice, you can boost your super balance by an additional $173,018.

THE SEVEN WINNING NUMBERS

INCOME	SUPER BALANCE (AGE 35)	SALARY PERCENTAGE CONTRIBUTED	CONTRIBUTION FREQUENCY	SUPER BALANCE (AGE 65)
$95,000	$80,000	10.5%	Quarterly	$551,658
$95,000	$80,000	15.5%	Quarterly	$724,676

Calculator Used: The ASIC Moneysmart Calculator [10]

Note: this scenario doesn't include pay rises, or future increases in the compulsory superannuation guarantee contribution cap. When you do your own calculations, different calculators will produce different results, dependent on the inputs and formulas used.

So, how much should you be putting into super?

You should be salary sacrificing at least 5% on top of what your employer contributes. Just go to your payroll department and ask them to do it.

Just relying on the compulsory 10.5% employer super guarantee (or even when it increases to 12%) isn't enough, especially if you want to retire before age 65.

And for those in a trade or doing a hard physical job, the 10.5% to 12% is definitely not enough because you will need to plan to retire by age 60. Your body may not allow you to continue working — even if you need to financially.

Speak to your adviser, accountant, or payroll department for help on how to salary sacrifice.

Summary for Winning Number 5
When you think about your super, think of the Winning Number 5. Salary sacrifice an extra 5% into your super. 5% a day keeps the doctor away!

THE SEVEN WINNING NUMBERS

"WELL MR. JONES, YOU'RE IN GREAT HEALTH FOR YOUR AGE. YOU'VE OBVIOUSLY BEEN SALARY SACRIFICING 5% INTO SUPER."

If you're self-employed

How to make contributions to super that are concessionally taxed.

Making 'personal' concessional contributions into super is the only option available if you are self-employed, and you are only paying yourself dividends or drawings and not a salary.

You can make your contribution to your super fund via BPAY or a direct debit from your bank account. If you do this, you will also need to:

1. Complete a tax deduction form
2. Give the form to your super fund
3. Make sure the super fund acknowledges the form
4. Tell your accountant who will claim the contribution as a tax deduction.

However, this alternative option is more complicated than salary sacrifice, and requires your direct action. It also requires a careful process.

If you, your accountant, or financial adviser doesn't follow this process correctly, you will not be able to claim your additional super contribution as a tax deduction.

If you are paid as an employee, it is much better just to automate the whole thing: salary sacrifice and forget about it.

Winning Number 120: How to invest your superannuation

Most people do not know how their super is invested.

For industry super funds, the default investment option is generally the Balanced option.

The Balanced option invests roughly 70% in growth assets and 30% in defensive income assets.

Growth assets include: shares (domestic and overseas), property (office towers and shopping centres etc.) and infrastructure (toll roads, airports, etc.).

Defensive/Income assets include: government and corporate bonds, money market deposits, mortgage-backed deposits, term deposits and cash.

Growth assets generate the greatest returns over the longer term, but are also the riskiest to invest in. Take a look at the share market, it's a roller coaster ride.

Defensive income assets give you very little opportunity to achieve capital growth (i.e., to enjoy an increase in the value of your investment). They provide income. Capital growth is low at best.

The Balanced option is not a bad investment option. That's why it's usually the default option.

It pre-mixes different asset classes for you, so you end up with a well-diversified portfolio all in one fund.

When you consider whether the Balanced option is appropriate for you, there are three things to consider:

1. The returns you make on the savings invested in your super, are heavily influenced by what assets you invest in. The more growth assets you invest in, the higher your expected return

over the long term. The more defensive income assets you invest in, the lower your expected return over the long term.

2. If you take on a lot of investment risk when you are retired, or near to retirement, by investing in mostly growth assets and the share market takes a big tumble, then you will have less to draw on to fund your retirement until the market recovers.

3. If you are too conservative when you are young, and have a large amount of your savings invested in defensive income assets, then you will suffer an 'opportunity cost' in the form of lower returns over the longer term, and end up saving less money for your retirement.

Being too conservative when you are younger increases your longevity risk.

What is longevity risk?

This is the risk that you will outlive your savings and run out of money. And life on just the Age Pension alone is not fun.

When it comes to building wealth via superannuation, your ability to withstand investment risk depends on two things:

1. Your investment time frame
2. Your life stage.

If you are 25 years of age, you graduated two years ago and are starting the climb up the corporate ladder, then you can't touch your super savings until age 60: that's 35 years away. And for the default retirement age of 65, that's 40 years away.

You have the ability at age 25 to invest all of your super savings in growth assets and take on substantial risk in order to get the best returns.

Why?

Because your lengthy investment time frame allows you to deal with several Global Financial Crises — plus several COVID outbreaks — and still have time to recover!

And why is it important to seek those high returns when you are young?

Because just a few percent extra on your investment return over 40 years, makes a massive difference to how much you will have saved and invested for your retirement.

Let's look at an example.

AGE	SALARY	STARTING BALANCE	AVERAGE RETURN	SUPER BALANCE AT AGE 65
25	$90,000	$50,000	7%	$601,951
25	$90,000	$50,000	9.5%	$1,072,333

Calculator used: ASIC Moneysmart Superannuation Calculator [11]

As you can see, earning a 2.5% p.a. higher return over 40 years can add over $470,000 to your savings for retirement!

If you do not want to leave your super invested in the Balanced option because you believe it is not suited to you, and you are seeking an asset allocation more tailored to your life stage, then the rule of 120 can be applied.

The Rule of 120: Take the Number 120 and subtract your age

The answer is the percentage of your superannuation savings that should be allocated to growth assets.

For example, if you are 25 years of age then the figure would be:

120 − 25 = invest 95% of your super funds in growth assets, and the balance of 5% in defensive income assets.

If you are 50 years of age, then the figure would be:

120 − 50 = invest 70% of your super funds in growth assets and 30% in defensive income assets.

As you can see, it is not until you are age 50 that you come back to the default Balanced option for your super savings. And at age 50, you still have 10 years left before you can access your super.

If you are a member of an industry super fund, choose the investment option closest to the asset allocation generated from the Rule of 120. Then every 5 years review this option by using the Rule of 120 again.

In reality, the Rule of 120 means that:

1. If you are in your late teens or 20s, you should be in the High Growth investment option.
2. By the age of 35, you should be considering switching to the Growth investment option and remaining in this investment option until at least the age of 45.
3. As you move past the age of 45, you should be considering a switch to the Balanced investment option. But if your super balance is low compared to your peers, you may want to consider remaining in the Growth option until you turn 50.

Be careful of investment option titles when looking at different industry super funds: 'Balanced' and 'Growth' mean different things to different super funds.

Below is a general guide on the percentage of growth and defensive assets for each named investment option:

- High Growth option = 95% or more in growth assets and 5% or less defensive income assets.
- Growth option = 85% growth assets and 15% defensive income assets.

- Balanced option = 70% growth assets and 30% defensive income assets.
- Moderate option = 50% growth assets and 50% defensive income assets.
- Conservative option = 30% growth assets and 70% defensive income assets.

How much money you have accumulated in super, and your planned retirement date will determine your next steps when it comes to investing your super savings.

A more conservative approach may be required from age 55 years onwards.

Summary for Winning Number 120

Take on more investment risk when you are young.

Why? Because the more you have saved for retirement, the less investment risk you need to take in retirement to generate the income you need to live on.

The more you have saved, the more conservative you can be in retirement. This is the stage of life where you should (and will) want to invest conservatively.

Invest according to your investment time frame and life stage, and make your money work harder for you.

The Rule of 120 and Your Superannuation Savings Summarised:

Under age 35	Invest in the High Growth option
Between 35 and 50	Invest in the Growth option
Over 50*	Invest in the Balanced option

Only apply the Rule of 120 until you reach age 55. Review your position then, as you may be only five years from retiring and accessing your super.

The Seven Winning Numbers again:

Winning Number 3
Establish 3 bank accounts to manage your hard-earned income and put it to good use.

Winning Number 20
Save 20 per cent of your income to clear any bad debt you may have accumulated, build an emergency fund, and then invest.

Winning Number 55
Aim to be mortgage-free by the time you are 55 so that you do not enter the 'Danger Zone' with home loan debt.

Winning Number 4
Take 4 steps to pay off your home loan as fast as humanly possible.

Winning Number 10
Save an additional 10 per cent and use those savings to make extra repayments on your home loan.

Winning Number 5
Salary sacrifice 5 per cent of your pre-tax salary into your superannuation fund, save on tax and make your super savings grow faster.

Winning Number 120
Invest your superannuation savings according to your age and life stage with the Rule of 120, and make your super savings work harder.

End of Part 1

Part 1 of this book has introduced you to the Foundations of Your Financial Future. It's a future where you take control of your finances to build your wealth, and be free to do the things in life that you enjoy, without having to worry about money.

You will make sacrifices when you apply The Seven Winning Numbers to your financial life. You are sacrificing your ability to spend money today, in order to have more money tomorrow.

For most people, having 'more money tomorrow' involves being debt-free and retiring well. And the sacrifice today will only involve you living within your means.

Help yourself to visualize the achievement of your financial goals by placing pictures or photos on your fridge that represent these goals. For example, a printout of:

- A photo of your dream holiday destination with the words: "my retirement" written on it.
- A photo of your house with the words: "I will be debt-free by 55" written on it.

Pictures like these will help you to see the future rewards from saving, budgeting, investing and being smarter with your money every day.

Visualizing your goals helps you remain committed to them.

PART 2

Building on your solid financial foundations

"An investment in knowledge pays the best interest."
— Benjamin Franklin (founding father of the United States)

Part 1 of this book touched on a range of financial topics such as saving, managing debt, as well as investing both inside and outside of superannuation. They need to be discussed in more detail.

Further, we need to introduce and discuss other topics such as personal insurance, estate planning and some of the financial decisions that self-employed people need to make.

All of the above are fundamental to helping you secure your financial future. As such, it is important to understand how these fundamentals work in order for you to make the best financial decisions.

You will have several options available to you when it comes to building wealth and protecting your family financially. Choosing which path to take can be difficult. In order to gain sufficient understanding of these fundamental principles, we need to see what is below the surface, and dive just a little deeper.

Part 2 is where we discuss these principles in more detail. As you read each chapter, highlight sentences, underline key words and make notes on the pages. Re-read parts to help let concepts sink in.

You may find some areas heavy reading, but it will be worth the effort. Speak to a licensed financial adviser for guidance if you are unsure about anything.

Let's dive in!

CHAPTER 3

Investing and building wealth

Compound interest

Compounding interest is one of the most important concepts you need to understand when investing. So, what do I mean by compounding?

Say you invest $100,000 in a term deposit paying 5% for 12 months.

At the end of one year, you get back your investment plus the interest = $105,000. Congratulations, you are $5,000 richer!

Say you then reinvest that $105,000 into another 12-month term deposit paying 5% interest. At the end of year 2, you get back $110,250. Great!

Guess how much interest you got for the second year? (Answer = $5,250).

That's more than the interest you earned in year 1 ($5,000).

Let's say you then reinvest that $110,250 into another 12-month term deposit paying 5%.

At the end of the third year, your investment is now worth $115,762.50. Awesome!

Guess how much interest you got for the third year?

(Answer = $5,512.50).

Hold on, that's more than the interest you earned in year 1 ($5,000) and year 2 ($5,250).

What's going on?

Well, you are now earning interest on the interest you invested back into a new term deposit. Your investment is now compounding (or snowballing)!

So, what would happen if you did this for 10 years?

YEAR	INVESTED AMOUNT	INTEREST RATE	INTEREST EARNED	BALANCE AT END OF TERM
1	$100,000	5%	$5,000	$105,000
2	$105,000	5%	$5,250	$110,250
3	$110,250	5%	$5,512	$115,762
4	$115,762	5%	$5,788	$121,550
5	$121,550	5%	$6,077	$127,628
6	$127,628	5%	$6,381	$134,009
7	$134,009	5%	$6,700	$140,710
8	$140,710	5%	$7,035	$147,745
9	$147,745	5%	$7,387	$155,132
10	$155,132	5%	$7,756	$162,889

At the end of year 10, your original $100,000 investment is worth $162,889!

So, what are the key inputs into making compounding work for you, so you can grow richer?

1. **Time:** It takes time to be effective. The longer your funds have been invested, the more your money grows.
2. **Return:** The higher the interest rate, the faster your money grows. Compounding is magnified by a higher return!
3. **Commitment:** Stay invested, never sell any part of your investment early. Even just a small withdrawal from your investment has a big impact.

Now, let's see what happens if we invest for 20 years:

YEAR	INVESTED AMOUNT	INTEREST RATE	INTEREST EARNED	BALANCED AT END OF TERM
1	$100,000	5%	$5,000	$105,000
5	$121,550	5%	$6,077	$127,628
10	$155,132	5%	$7,756	$162,889
15	$197,993	5%	$9,899	$207,892
20	$252,695	5%	$12,634	$265,329

At the end of year 15, your money has more than doubled with an interest rate of 5%.

And at the end of year 20, your original investment of $100,000 is worth $265,329.

More of your investment is now the interest you have earned rather than the original amount you put in:

- Original Invested Amount = $100,000
- Total Interest Earned = $165,329.

Let's now increase the interest rate.

We are going to use an average return you could realistically expect to achieve by investing in the share market in Australia over the long term: 8.5%.

YEAR	INVESTED AMOUNT	INTEREST RATE	INTEREST EARNED	BALANCED AT END OF TERM
1	$100,000	8.5%	$8,500	$108,500
5	$138,585	8.5%	$11,779	$150,365
10	$208,385	8.5%	$17,712	$226,098
15	$313,340	8.5%	$26,633	$339,974
20	$471,156	8.5%	$40,048	$511,204

Instead of having $265,329 at the end of year 20, you now have over half a million dollars! This is because the average rate of return every year has been higher.

Note your return in Year 20: your investment increases by over $40,000 in one year alone. Compare this to the return you achieved in Year 1: $8,500. The longer you remain invested, the better compounding works.

The above scenarios are simplistic. I have not taken into consideration the ups and downs of the share market (the good and bad years) or taxation.

However, you get my point! Compounding works and it works well.

So why don't people do this? Honestly, because most people can't be bothered.

Or, if they do invest, they sell their investment early. They don't allow the compounding to work by investing for the longer term!

Compounding takes time, and it takes commitment.

The longer you invest for, the better.

Investing in the share market

Investing in shares (or equities or stocks as they may be called — they are all the same thing) is not for the faint-hearted. Watching the share market go up and down can be like watching your kid ride the roller coaster at Dreamworld: nauseating!

However, the share market is how the richest investor in history made his wealth: the one and only Warren Buffett.

If you wish to embark on a journey of self-discovery by conducting your own research, and build your own portfolio through investing in shares directly, then you need to be a pupil of Warren Buffett. Look no further, as there is no one else like him, and likely never will be again. He remains way ahead of the game.

Let's consider two common ways to approach investing on the Australian share market:

1. Actively build your own portfolio of shares over time, and manage it — personally — on an ongoing basis. Either reinvest your dividends or if you are seeking capital growth, buy and sell where and when you see value.

2. Invest passively via a managed fund such as the Vanguard Australian Shares Index Fund[12] (an Exchange Traded Fund or ETF). Reinvest all of the dividends you receive back into the fund. And invest funds quarterly from your Savings Account into this same ETF.

Replicating Warren Buffett's success or even 'beating the market' consistently year in year out is very difficult. Even professional fund managers struggle with this task. What Warren Buffett demonstrates to us, is how important shares are as an asset class when it comes to creating wealth.

For most of us, Approach 2 is more suitable than Approach 1, and Approach 2 can still produce a very profitable outcome for any investor over the long term.

Why would you consider a fund like the aforementioned Vanguard Australian Shares Index ETF?

- Shares in the fund can easily be bought through any online broker, just like a normal share in a company.
- The management fees charged by the fund manager are dirt-cheap.
- The fund invests in the top 300 stocks on the Australian share market by size and liquidity, and it is reasonably diversified.
- The fund pays dividends quarterly, and allows you to compound your investment four times a year.
- The fund rarely buys or sells stocks, so transaction costs are low and capital gains tax events are low.
- The fund pays franking credits* (see below) in addition to dividends.
- You can automatically reinvest your dividends, and avoid paying brokerage.
- The Vanguard Australian Shares Index ETF is traded frequently on the share market: there are many buyers and sellers. Thus, the buy and sell prices listed for shares in this ETF, are generally closer together. This sharper pricing is of benefit to you as an investor.

*What are franking credits?

Franking credits (also called imputation credits) are in effect, a tax refund.

An Australian company with an annual turnover of more than $50 million pays a tax rate of 30% on its profits.[13]

That same Australian company pays its shareholders/investors a dividend from its after-tax profits. Those dividends then get added to the investor's taxable income. What seems to be the problem with that? Well, that means the Australian Tax Office (ATO) is effectively taxing those profits twice:

- Firstly, when the company pays tax on the profits.
- Secondly, when you pay income tax on the very same (already taxed) profits, which are then distributed to you.

So, former Prime Minister and Treasurer Paul Keating decided to pass a law that allows the refund of company tax to Australian resident investors: i.e., you and me. That tax refund is called a franking credit. Thanks Paul!

Franking credits make investing in Australian companies much more tax effective.

Note: Non–residents (i.e. those who live outside of Australia) are not eligible for a franking credit tax refund.

Right, let's get back to investing in shares.

Question:

If I don't want to buy shares myself, or if I don't have the time to manage a portfolio of stocks, is the Vanguard Australia Shares Index ETF my only option?

Answer:

No! You have a number of options including:
- Listed investment companies (LICs)
- Unlisted actively managed funds
- Other exchange-traded funds.

We'll now look at each of these options in more detail.

Listed Investment Companies (LICs)

LICs have been around for a long time. They are a company that invests in other companies. LICs have a management team that actively makes the investment decisions on your behalf.

Because they operate under a corporate structure, they do not have to distribute profits to shareholders like trusts do. An LIC can retain profits indefinitely and pay dividends whenever they want.

LICs must pay tax on those profits every year of course, but by holding onto some of the profits, they can pay dividends to shareholders in lean times as well as good. This helps to ensure that shareholders who rely on their dividends rarely go without.

When someone wants to invest in an LIC, they buy shares in the LIC on the share market, via an online stock broker like Commsec or Nabtrade.

When they want to sell, they sell the shares the same way. Remaining investors are not impacted by other investors buying and selling, like they are for exchange-traded and unlisted managed funds (see the next section).

Sometimes the share price of an LIC is worth more or less than the value of the companies they have invested in.

Why would that be?

Because investors are willing to pay more or less for the shares, based on their opinion of the LIC's management.

In other words, some LICs shares are trading at a premium (or discount) to their net assets because investors think the managers are either great (or lousy) stock pickers. But sometimes, investors just get it plain wrong.

The fees charged by the managers of an LIC vary, but are usually fairly low compared to actively managed funds.

Unlisted actively managed funds

An unlisted actively managed fund is exactly what it sounds like. It is a fund where many investors have their savings pooled together and invested. The fund manager invests the money, and charges investors a fee for doing so.

The fund itself is not listed on the stock market. So, if you want to withdraw your savings, you have to request that part or all of the investment is redeemed and returned to you.

The fund manager will either use a cash reserve, or have to sell some investments to pay you back.

Both investing in, and withdrawing from, a managed fund can take some time. It may also require paperwork to be signed and returned.

Unlisted managed funds are therefore not as 'liquid' as listed LICs or ETFs.

It is important to note that if the fund manager ever has to sell investments to pay out former investors, it may trigger capital gains tax events. Remaining investors may be negatively impacted as a result, and be lumped with extra tax to pay.

Unlisted managed funds are often actively managed where the fund manager tries to beat the market index, but they can also invest passively by merely copying the market index.

If the fund is actively managed, the fees charged by fund managers will be a lot higher than those charged by an LIC or ETF.

It should be noted that most active fund managers who try and beat the market generally don't. They fail and underperform.

This is because their fees are too high, which wipes out their superior gains. Or they just make bad investment decisions.

Many active fund managers feel compelled to make investment decisions regularly, so they look like they are doing something to earn their higher fee. But these decisions may not necessarily add true value to your portfolio, just extra cost.

Unlike LIC's, all profits made by an unlisted managed fund have to be distributed to investors every year. They can't be retained to pay dividends in lean years.

Exchange-traded funds (ETFs)

ETFs are a more recent invention when compared to LICs or unlisted managed funds. Instead of having to complete application forms to invest, you can just buy shares in an exchange-traded fund like any other share on the share market.

Buying and selling shares in an ETF is quick and easy.

Most ETFs track an index, and are not actively managed to try and 'beat the market'.

LIC's, unlisted managed funds and ETFs don't just invest in Australian shares, they can also invest in the following:
- overseas shares
- commercial property — offices, warehouses, retail shops, and other commercial premises
- infrastructure — water utilities, toll roads, rail, airports and shipping ports
- agriculture products and other soft (grown) commodities
- oil, gas, metals, coal
- gold and other precious metals.

You will need to do some research, and look at which investment option suits you best.

I prefer ETFs because:

- They are very liquid (i.e. ETF shares can be bought and sold very quickly): if I want to get my money out fast I can.
- The cost of investing via an ETF is very low (i.e. their fees are cheap). High fees have a big negative impact on returns.
- They are simple and easy to understand.
- It is a very easy way to diversify and spread your investment "eggs" in many baskets.
- You can set up an automatic dividend reinvestment plan, and avoid paying any brokerage.
- The price you pay for a share in an ETF matches the value of the investments they hold, unlike an LIC.

However, the one key negative of an ETF when compared to owning shares directly, is the inability to time when you incur a capital gain. An ETF fund manager may sell a stock holding held inside the fund and pass this capital gain onto you unexpectedly. You may therefore incur a taxable event in a financial year not suitable to you, resulting in a larger tax bill.

Should you own the stock directly (not via an investment fund of any sort), you can control when you sell the stock and when you generate the taxable capital gain.

For many Aussies, when it comes to investing in shares, it will only be the Australian share market that they focus on.

What are the positives of investing in Australian shares?

1. It is easy to diversify across different companies through a portfolio of shares.
2. Shares are generally very liquid: you can sell your investment on the share market and have your funds in your bank account in a few business days.

3. You can make money when your investment goes up in value (capital growth) and from any dividend income paid to you.

4. Australian companies generally pay higher dividends, compared to overseas companies[14].

5. Dividend payments tend to be steadier than the value of the stocks themselves.

6. The brokerage paid to buy or sell shares is very low, compared to the costs of buying or selling a residential investment property.

7. You don't have to worry about the running costs of your investment, compared to investing in a residential investment property.

8. Fluctuations in the value of the Australian Dollar against other currencies won't impact the value of your investment, compared to investing directly into overseas companies.

The negatives of investing in Australian shares are:

1. The Australian share market is a roller coaster ride over the short and medium-term: the value of your portfolio can go up and down markedly.

2. Companies do not have to pay dividends, they can be reduced or even stopped: if a company is in trouble, they quite often reduce or cancel dividends.

3. The Australian share market is small, and not as well diversified, when compared to the American, European or British stock markets.

4. If you want to borrow to invest in shares, the dividend income is not included in any calculation made by the bank when it decides whether to lend you the money or not.

5. Australian listed companies are incentivised through our tax system (franking credits) to pay larger dividends. As a result, an investor in Australian companies will generally have less control over when they earn taxable income, and therefore pay tax on their earnings.

6. Only by investing directly in low dividend growth companies, can you control when you will earn a taxable income (capital gain), through timing when you sell your shares at a profit. Taking this approach may significantly reduce the number of Australian companies you deem suitable as an investment and prove restrictive.

Diversification: Spreading your eggs in many baskets

One consideration when it comes to investing in shares or managed funds, is the size and composition of the Australia Securities Exchange (ASX).

The Australian share market is tiny in the global context; it comprises only about 2% of the world's listed companies. It is also dominated by a few companies that dig stuff out of the ground, and four big banks[15].

If you want to truly diversify, then you need to invest overseas. If you take yourself seriously as a stock picker, you are probably doing this already.

If you take the main United States stock market (the New York Stock Exchange) for example: it is 16 times larger than the ASX[16]. A well-diversified investor would most certainly be investing in companies listed on the New York Stock Exchange (NYSE) because there are a huge number of large, world-leading companies listed on it.

These companies listed on the NYSE are involved in making life-saving drugs, mobile phones, computer software & hardware, electric cars, heavy machinery and social media providers. These are sectors of the global economy that we just don't have in Australia.

A diversified investor would also be invested in other regions and countries around the world such as the Britain and the European Union.

Question:	So how can you invest in overseas companies easily?
Answer:	Through a managed fund that invests overseas for you.
Question:	OK, so how much should I invest overseas?
Answer:	Rule of thumb = 60% Overseas and 40% in Australia.

This rule of thumb is based on the following:

- You are a resident of Australia and can receive franking credits to make investing in Australian shares more tax effective.

- Returns from overseas shares are earned in other currencies, and these returns need to be converted back to Australian dollars before they can be paid to you. Fluctuations in exchange rates can impact returns.

- The small size of the Australian share market compared to overseas share markets.

The 60:40 ratio favours overseas stocks. It is an acknowledgement of the small size of the Australian share market, and its lack of exposure to some sectors of the global economy. However, the ratio also retains a reasonable exposure to Australian stocks, given the tax-effectiveness of franked dividends delivered by Australian companies.

I have seen the recommended ratio of overseas to Australian shares vary significantly among advisers. But I believe remaining near the middle ground of 50:50 — skewed toward the rest of the world (which represents about 98% of the global stock market) — is best.

Companies like Vanguard make investing to a ratio very easy.

If you were to invest 60% of your savings in the Vanguard MSCI Index International Shares ETF[17] (ASX code VGS) and then 40% into the Vanguard Australian Shares Index ETF[18] (ASX code VAS), you would be invested in about 1500 overseas companies and 300 Australian companies.

This is one of the simplest ways to invest in shares and be well diversified.

Diversification is not only achieved on the stock market by investing globally and across different sectors of the world economy, but also by investing in other assets such as:

1. Property — Australian and overseas
2. Infrastructure — Australian and overseas
3. Bonds and fixed interest — Australian and overseas.

You can create your own portfolio of diversified Australian and overseas investments in shares, property, infrastructure, bonds and mortgage-backed securities.

You can do this by investing in a fund that specialises in each asset class, and put the funds together to form your portfolio.

Or, to help you make things simpler and easier, companies like Vanguard, iShares, Betashares or VanEck also do this for you. They have funds that invest in a pre-mixed portfolio. These funds are simple, low cost and well diversified, similar to an industry super fund investment option.

Shop around to see what is out there. Or make an appointment with a licensed financial planner to discuss further.

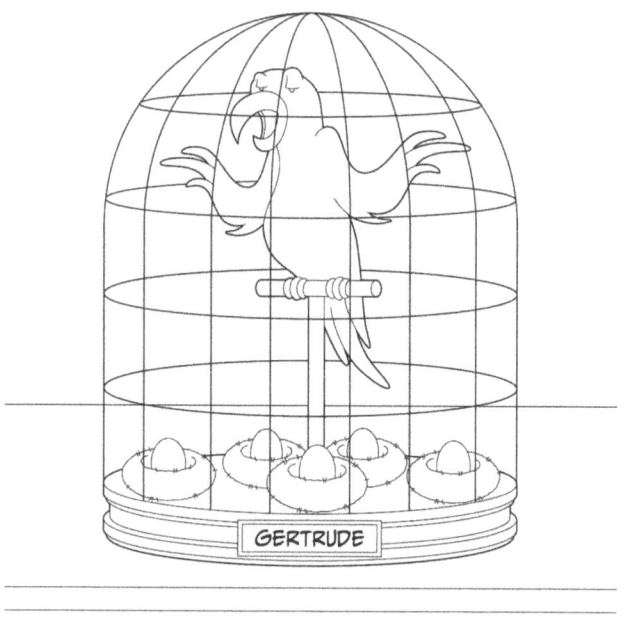

"HEY, DON'T JUDGE. IT'S HOW I MANAGE RISK."

Let's go back and consider the 20% you are saving every fortnight.

So, you have paid out all of your bad debt.

You have saved an emergency fund in your Savings Account.

You are happy because you have worked hard and have saved up six months of your household living expenses (including your mortgage repayments). You feel secure in the knowledge that these funds are sitting there in your offset account, reducing the amount of interest you pay on your mortgage.

It's now time to put your savings to good use. This is where you start your first investment outside of super.

Let's say you purchase $2,000 of shares in the Vanguard Australian Shares Index ETF* for example.[19]

You then instruct Vanguard to reinvest your quarterly distributions, because you understand the benefits of compounding.

You are happy because you don't pay any brokerage on the reinvested dividends.

Instead of paying the dividends, Vanguard just issues you with more shares.

You then set up a quarterly direct debit to your Vanguard Personal Investment Account from your Savings Account. You will use these funds to purchase more shares in the Vanguard Australian Shares Index ETF.

So how much should you put in every quarter?

If you are saving 20% of your wage, then you could invest three-quarters of this into Vanguard. *(You can obviously vary this amount to suit your needs and goals).*

The remaining one-quarter of your wage that you save, can remain in your Savings Account to further build your cash savings.

Whenever you invest in growth assets, you should always ensure you have funds saved in cash for emergencies.

You should never have to touch your investment in an emergency. You have your cash savings for that!

Take a look at the below diagram, to see how this saving and investment strategy works when added to the 'Winning Numbers 3 and 20' example outlined in Chapter 2.

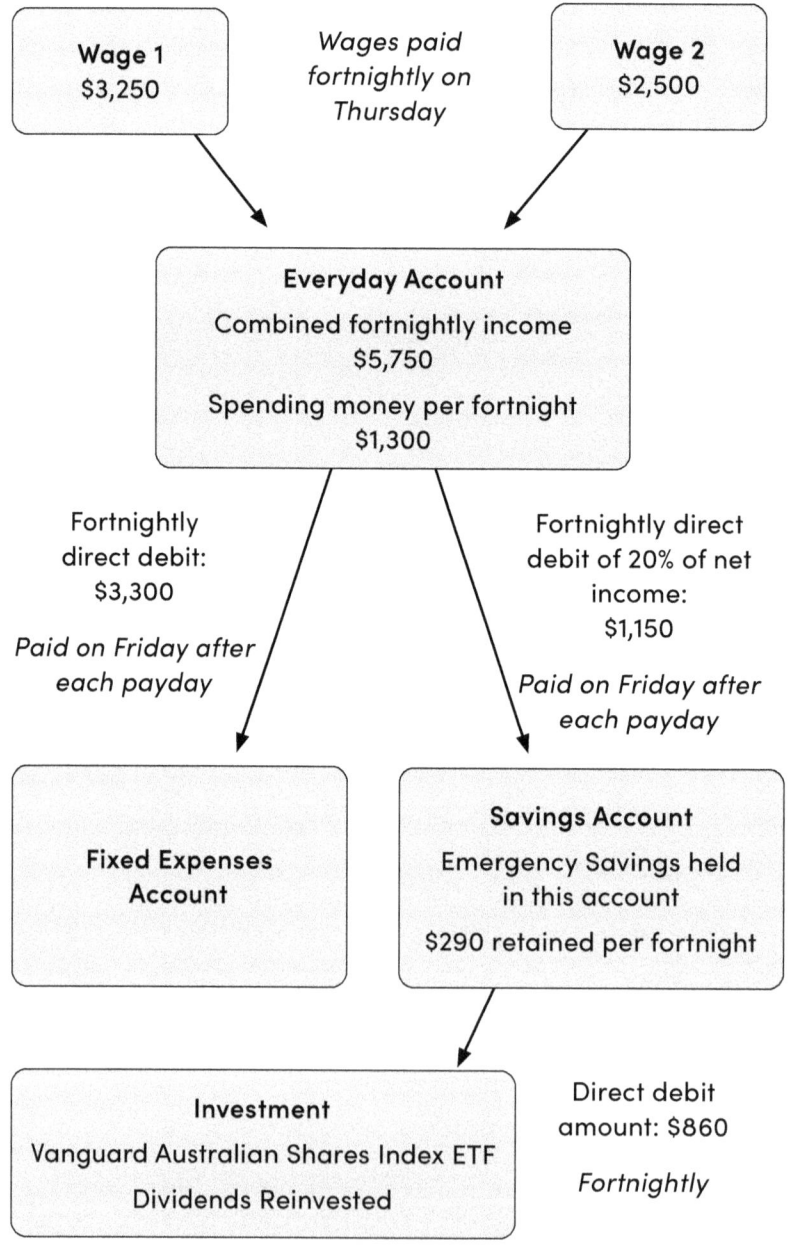

Note: I have used the Vanguard Australian Shares Index ETF and other Vanguard funds as examples in this book for the benefit of overseas readers who will be familiar with the brand given its global reach.

This is not an endorsement of Vanguard as a company or its funds. Whilst overseas readers may be familiar with other index fund providers such as Blackrock's iShares or VanEck for example, they will not be familiar with Australian based index fund managers such as Betashares etc. Particularly Australians who have lived overseas for quite some time.

Overseas and Australian readers will need to conduct their own research into the index fund providers that operate in their respective country, and select those funds they believe is best for them.

There are many index fund providers out there.

Let's work through another scenario where the saving and investment strategy is applied over 20 years.

Ben is 30 years old and earns $90,000 per year. He does not want to work until age 60, he wants to retire sooner than that, but he knows he can't access his super until he's at least age 60.

He has a home loan and an offset account. He has followed all of The Seven Winning Numbers, and he saves 20% of his income in his offset account.

He needs a solution to his problem. The solution is to build an investment outside of super that he has access to, and which is large enough to fund his lifestyle until he can access his super.

He decides to invest an initial $2,000 in the Vanguard Australian Shares Index ETF[20] and has set up a monthly direct debit via his Vanguard Personal Investor Account for $830.

He also reinvests any dividends he receives back into more shares.

You can see in the following table that I have included good years, bad years and average years and not just simply taken an average return, and applied to every year.

This is a truer representation of what you will experience as an investor: the share market can be a roller-coaster ride. In some years, you will see your investment fall.

I have also separated capital growth and dividend income.

The value of your investment will go up and down a lot more than the dividends you receive, especially from an index fund that invests in hundreds of Australian companies. This is normal.

Note: I have made a number of assumptions when creating this spreadsheet. I haven't included the impact of income tax in this calculation, but I have also not included the benefit of franking credits paid, which can help to offset tax implications. To include tax and franking credits would be distracting, and not really value add to the main aim here: to demonstrate how to build wealth.

The total average annual return is 9.04% for this scenario (4.57% capital growth plus 4.47% dividend income). This is a typical rate of return from Australian shares over the longer term.[21]

Over 25 years, Ben will build up an investment fund worth well over three quarters of a million dollars. This is in addition to his super fund, which will also be growing.

This is realistic for Ben to achieve, but it will take 25 years and commitment. Ben will have to go without for a long time: fewer holidays, less fun and less spending money. But is his goal of retiring before age 60 looking achievable? You bet it is!

YEAR	CAPITAL GAIN/LOSS	DIVIDEND INCOME	NET INCOME FOR RE-INVESTMENT	CAPITAL GROWTH	INVESTMENT VALUE
1	14.1%	3.95%	$472	$1,682	$14,115
2	-7.5%	3.19%	$768	$-1,817	$23,026
3	-2.4%	3.60%	$1,186	$-778	$33,394
4	7.0%	4.76%	$2,065	$3,044	$48,463
5	15.6%	5.05%	$2,950	$9,128	$70,502
6	26.3%	5.46%	$4,396	$21,134	$105,993
7	11.1%	4.88%	$5,660	$12,898	$134,512
8	27.8%	4.94%	$7,137	$40,109	$191,719
9	-30.2%	3.16%	$6,371	$-60,986	$147,064
10	3.3%	5.21%	$8,188	$5,171	$170,384
11	-3.3%	3.95%	$7,130	$-5,955	$181,518
12	-12.6%	3.92%	$7,506	$-24,182	$174,802
13	9.1%	5.32%	$9,825	$16,885	$211,473
14	18.4%	5.26%	$11,640	$40,639	$273,713
15	1.3%	4.47%	$12,672	$3,595	$299,941
16	-5.1%	4.42%	$13,699	$-15,759	$307,840
17	8.6%	4.90%	$15,566	$27,343	$360,710
18	4.3%	4.68%	$17,342	$16,082	$404,095
19	9.4%	4.67%	$19,325	$38,769	$472,150
20	7.9%	4.69%	$22,597	$37,995	$542,704
21	-12.0%	3.33%	$18,416	$-66,336	$504,743
22	15.2%	5.01%	$25,789	$78,119	$618,612
23	10.1%	4.54%	$28,526	$63,228	$720,327
24	-9.4%	4.31%	$31,501	$-68,646	$693,141
25	7.5%	4.11%	$28,883	$52,910	$784,895
AVERAGE RETURN	4.57%	4.47%			

With over half a million dollars saved by age 50, and three-quarters of a million dollars by age 55, it's looking very realistic. Ben can now plan to retire before the age of 60 with more certainty.

He will keep building his portfolio until that time, when he plans to transition to part-time work. While this means his salary will also reduce, he will stop reinvesting his dividends and start to pay himself the quarterly distribution instead. He will also receive franking credits in his tax return every year.

This wealth creation strategy does involve you taking on investment risk. But it does not involve you having to borrow any money to invest with: It is an investment strategy where no gearing is required. (I talk more about gearing in Chapter 4). And don't forget, part of this strategy is to have and always maintain cash savings for emergencies.

What are some considerations with investing primarily in Australian shares via an ETF?

- When it's time to retire, you can simply stop reinvesting your dividends, and have them paid to your bank account to fund your retirement along with your franking credits. You do not have to sell your shares.

- If you have other sources of income such as rent from an investment property, savings and/or super, the total investment income you receive may be more than enough to pay all of your living expenses.

- Being able to receive higher dividends and franking credits makes Australian index funds more attractive for those investors seeking regular income, rather than mostly capital growth.

- Higher dividends paid by Australian companies are a steadier (less volatile) and tax-effective way to reward shareholders.
- Higher dividends also allow you to compound your investment through automatic dividend reinvestment.
- Without investing in overseas shares, you will not be as well diversified.

What are some considerations when investing in both overseas and Australian shares via an ETF?

- Including overseas companies improves your diversification, which means less investment risk.
- Overseas shares (in particular American tech companies) have experienced substantial growth in the last decade. Some would argue that these types of companies have the potential to grow faster than most Australian companies because of the types of industries they are in: disruptive and transformational technology.
- Overseas companies generally tend to focus more on capital growth than dividends when rewarding investors.

If you sell down funds that invest in overseas stocks in the future, you may as a result, pay more in capital gains tax when compared to investing primarily in Australian Share Index ETF's.

You can however, select the financial year when you do sell, which may be in a year where your working income is low in order to reduce the tax implications.

Fear and greed

> *"Be fearful when others are greedy, and greedy when others are fearful."*
> — Warren Buffett

I once struck up a conversation about a client's portfolio, and how we were going to continue to build it moving forward. My client was a long-term investor. The market had fallen by a reasonable amount during the previous six months (post-COVID inflation crash).

I believed it was a buying opportunity for an investor seeking to outperform the market over the long term, as well as to invest with reduced downside risk.

His response was that he did not want to continue to build on his share portfolio further, until the market had recovered after the recent fall.

I explained to him what his response meant with an analogy: it was like going into a car dealership looking for a new car. When he arrived there, a sale was on and cars were 20% off their normal retail price, but he decided to wait until the sale was over and paid full price instead.

In this case, fear made my client decline to continue to build his portfolio after prices had fallen. He feared a further loss in the value of his portfolio.

But guess what, when you buy into a good quality company, with good management, and a good competitive advantage for a lower price, the risk of the stock falling has actually reduced.

Why?

Because the share price has already fallen!

As the share price falls, the stock becomes better value for money. The upside potential increases, and the downside potential reduces.

It is theoretically less risky to buy into a good quality company at a lower price, than at a higher price.

The exact opposite is also true.

People will see the market rise significantly and then want to buy shares. The problem is the ship has already sailed. Someone else has profited, not you.

After a significant rise in the share market, the risk of a fall in the market increases. You may actually be buying the stock when it is overpriced, and in doing so lining someone else's pockets, rather than your own.

Success in the share market depends heavily on controlling your emotions, having conviction in your research, and committing to the companies you buy at a good price.

If you cannot be clinical and emotionless when investing, then you cannot be a successful investor. You most certainly should not be buying and selling shares yourself.

Investing via an index fund, reinvesting all your dividends, investing on a regular basis and not getting heavily involved in the investment decision-making is all you should be doing, to build wealth over the long term.

By doing so, you are automating your investing, and leaving your emotions at the door.

A sound approach to buying shares

If you are determined to build your own portfolio, then consider this approach.

Conduct your research on which listed companies you believe are great companies, regardless of their share price.

Then place these companies on a watch list, and wait until their share price represents good value. In other words, buy when the company is below its intrinsic value by a margin.

What have you just done when you do? You have got your brand-new car from the dealership — for a 20% discount.

I only need two words to support this argument when it comes to buying a stock this way: Warren Buffett. Just look at his success. You can listen to Warren Buffett on YouTube. You can also buy books on how to follow his approach to investing. You can search for articles on the internet that will explain how he invests as well.

So much of successfully buying shares is patience, temperament and emotional intelligence.

It is rare for someone as successful as Warren Buffet to share the secrets of his success, and so willingly.

Take advantage of the fact that he also possesses the humility to talk about his failures. When it comes to learning how to invest on the share market, it is best to learn from the best. Why would you listen to second-best or anyone else (including me for that matter)?

It takes considerable time to research companies sufficiently, in order to know what you are investing in. During this research, you should be reading the company annual report — cover to cover.

You should be diving into the financials of the listed company, and at the same time pretending that you are buying the whole business with your life's savings.

If you struggle to understand company accounting, then I recommend reading books such as Warren Buffett and the Interpretation of Financial Statements by Mary Buffett and David Clark.[22] Once you have read it, and similar books you will feel a lot more confident researching companies.

Investing in shares, by building your own portfolio, takes a substantial amount of time. You will need to put the effort into research, and continually monitoring your investments.

Financial commentators talk about the fact that 'time in the market, not timing, is important'.

That's simplistic, and you know it.

This formula does not suit building your own portfolio of stocks. You won't be building wealth via compounding, you will more likely be building it via capital growth.

It may take a few years to actually build your portfolio into the one you want. Remember, you only buy stocks when they represent good value.

Time in the market is for when you invest in an index fund, reinvest all your dividends and make regular investments from savings. When you do, you are relying on compounding for success.

In some years, I have seen the value of shares in my Australian share index fund fall, but at the same time I've also seen the total value of my portfolio being maintained because I reinvest all dividend payments automatically, and receive additional shares instead.

Your portfolio won't be invested in 300 Australian stocks or 1,500 overseas stocks if you don't invest in index funds. In reality, you may have only 10 to 25 companies in your portfolio.

You will be much more reliant on each individual stock than a passive investor, and therefore be heavily reliant on your stock-picking skills and timing.

Timing equals buying at the right price. This is how you will manage the downside risks of investing for capital gain, as opposed to high dividend yields.

Finally, consider if you would be better off putting more hours in at work, instead of building your own portfolio of stocks. As the old saying goes time is money, and you need to consider how much money you could earn an hour in your trade or job.

Would you be better off earning that additional income, and investing it regularly in an index fund instead?

Will you make more money selecting stocks yourself, above and beyond average market index returns that justifies the time you put into your research?

For most people, a second job or more hours in their normal job will be a more lucrative path.

Your circle of trust

> *"If an idiot were to tell you the same story every day for a year, you would end by believing it."*
>
> — Horace Mann (American education pioneer and reformer)

It is important to be selective in who you talk to about wealth creation.

Listen to (and seek knowledge from) people who have been successful in building wealth.

Bounce ideas off only those who you trust and respect, not with whoever happens to be at the pub on a Thursday afternoon.

Listening to people who have been stupid with their money, and who continue to make bad financial decisions, can end up influencing you to make similar bad decisions.

If you allow yourself to be influenced by poor money managers, you may suffer a similar fate: being poor. The only exception is when they share their mistakes with you, in the hope you don't make the same mistakes too.

When it comes to buying shares, going with a tip from a mate at work just doesn't cut it.

Conduct your own research, join an investment club, or speak to someone who has been successful investing in shares.

Learn, listen, and build your knowledge and understanding, so you can make better, more-informed decisions with your money.

Any financial engagement you have with someone should never have a sales pitch included.

Avoid wealth-creation seminars that are fronts for selling you a residential property that they have chosen, or a 'tax-effective' investment in a timber plantation. Following advice from seminars like these is a sure-fire way to end up poor.

And never, ever engage with anyone who approaches you unsolicited. In other words, anyone cold-calling or contacting you with a 'wealth-creation strategy'. Hang up and ignore them.

I cannot emphasise this enough!

It is an unfortunate reality that it is easier to con someone out of their life savings, than it is to convince them they are being conned.

Managing people's money is an incredible responsibility and a serious business. I have met more unethical people during my career as a financial adviser, than at any other stage of my adult life. And I am not talking about my clients. It pays to be cautious!

"HAVE I GOT A PROPERTY FOR YOU TO INVEST IN! WITH SEA VIEWS LIKE THAT, HOW CAN YOU GO WRONG?... LEAVE EVERYTHING, INCLUDING FINANCE, TO US. YOU'RE IN SAFE HANDS!"

Whose name should you invest in?

If you are part of a couple, consider which of you earns less from your working income, and is thus on a lower marginal tax rate.

Also consider the likelihood that whichever one of you is currently earning less, will continue to earn less into the future, and thus continue to be taxed at that lower marginal tax rate.

If you decide to invest outside of superannuation, invest in the name of the person on the lower marginal tax rate.

Less will go to the taxman and more will go to you!

If you are both on the same marginal tax rate and expect this to remain the case over the longer term, then you can just invest outside of super in joint names.

If you are in doubt, speak to your accountant about the tax implications of investing, and they will guide you on how to do it in a tax-effective manner.

There is an alternative for those on higher marginal tax rates, and that is to invest via an insurance bond.

Insurance bonds

Insurance bonds (also called investment bonds) possess the combined characteristics of an insurance policy and an investment. They are a great product to use for investing because they are second only to superannuation in terms of being tax effective.

They allow you to invest in the same way as you would do in your own name, except via a separate legal entity. Insurance bonds pay no more than 30% tax on profits, and you do not have to declare any income you earn on an insurance bond because it is not in your name.

If you are in the top two marginal tax brackets (i.e., 37% or 45%)[23], then investing in insurance bonds is a serious consideration for you.

You can 'set and forget' by investing a simple lump sum once into an insurance bond. Or you can invest a small amount initially, and make regular investments. Your contributions over a year can be up to 25% more than you contributed the previous year.

You can access your savings in an insurance bond at any time. But if you do access your funds within 10 years, there are tax implications.

After you have held your insurance bond for at least 10 years, you can withdraw your money tax-free. You can therefore turn it into a tax–paid retirement fund if you wish.

There is also the insurance component. Insurance bonds have a life insured, a policy owner and a beneficiary.

If you nominate a beneficiary such as your child or grandchild, then the insurance bond is cashed in and paid to them directly and discreetly if the insured person dies, just like a life insurance policy. And the beneficiary receives the proceeds of the bond tax–free.

An insurance bond with a nominated beneficiary is not an estate asset, and is therefore not dealt with via your will. (More on estate assets later).

Normally, if you invest in your own name, and you own that asset for more than 12 months, any capital gain (increase in value) on that investment is discounted by 50% if you sell, when being assessed for capital gains tax. This is very beneficial.

However, the one negative about an insurance bond is that they are not allowed to use the 50% capital gains tax discount. For that reason, your after-tax return may be higher if you invest in your own name, rather than via an insurance bond. This of course depends on what you invest in.

You will have several investment options available with insurance bonds, but those options may be more limited when compared to investing in your own name.

You should again do your research, and keep a very close eye on the fees charged by insurance bond providers. These additional fees (charged on top of investing normally in your own name) will have a negative impact on your returns over the long term.

Not many people use insurance bonds, as they are a more complicated investment product. There are rules you need to follow to make it worthwhile to invest in one.

Insurance bonds should only really be considered by people who:

- want to bequeath their wealth to specific individuals with certainty, or
- are in the top marginal tax rates, or both.

Investing in residential property

Australians love property. Bricks and mortar are pretty much the 'go–to' investment for an Aussie, and those who don't have an investment property probably want one. Residential property is easy to understand. It is tangible (you can touch and see it).

The residential property sector is vast and can be broken down into many subsectors:

a) houses, townhouses and apartments

b) owner-occupied, tenanted and holiday homes

c) long-term rentals and holiday/short-term rentals

d) large cities, provincial cities and regional towns

e) inner-city and outer-city suburbs.

The list goes on and on.

The positives of investing in residential property are:

- If someone lives in your investment property, they have to pay rent. It is not optional.
- You have the potential to receive rental income plus an increase in the value of your property.

- 75% to 80% of the rent is included in your income when a bank considers your loan application, helping you to afford to borrow and invest in property.
- A bank will use all of the value of the residential property when taking it as security for your loan.
- A bank will lend you up to 70% to 80% of the total value of all property used as security for the loan.

The negatives of investing in residential property are:

- If you are heavily reliant on the tenant paying you rent in order to service your loan repayments, any tenant default will immediately put you in financial stress if you have no savings set aside.
- Property is not a liquid investment. It may take quite some time to sell, and you cannot sell part of your property investment.
- It is one big egg in one big basket. You will need to conduct your research thoroughly and buy the right type of property, in the right location.
- It costs a lot of money to buy and sell property: stamp duty, legal fees, lender fees and agent fees.
- Property running costs can eat into rental returns: land tax, body corporate fees, repairs, insurance, rates, water and sewerage.

Sometimes familiarity with property can result in investor overconfidence. Just because you understand and can see your investment, does not make you an expert.

I have always found it fascinating that people can lose money on a residential property investment, but be quite willing to invest in property again. Yet if they lose money on the share market, they will often never consider buying shares again.

So where should you look for a rental property to buy?

Location, location, location:

- People need to live close to where they work. Select an area with a good variety of decent jobs and a well-diversified economy that includes hospitals, universities, government agencies and financial services.
- Close to good schools: parents value convenience, a short school run, and will often want to buy a home within the catchment of a well-regarded school.
- Close to conveniences: shops, a doctor's surgery, a pharmacy and restaurants.
- Access to various modes of transport to work: trains, buses and commuter motorways (although not too close).
- Nearby parks, lakes, the beach and other niceties.
- Avoid busy roads, heavy traffic, high-voltage power lines and noisy, smelly industrial locations.

The worst experiences I have witnessed in residential property investing, were people who bought in mining towns during the commodity boom.

They bought properties in small regional towns that were heavily reliant on one employment source: mining.

They bought at the top of the market at inflated prices. When the commodity boom collapsed, these people had multiple properties worth half what they paid for them, and they could not find tenants. If they did, they paid a fraction of what was previously paid in rent at the height of the boom.

In the end, many of these people had to sell their own home plus their investment properties to pay back their bank. They were wiped out, and will never recover.

Cryptocurrencies

It is almost guaranteed that a conversation will start about cryptocurrencies such as Bitcoin at a barbeque somewhere in Australia this weekend.

"Have you bought any?"

"My brother's son's best mate has made a killing on Bitcoin! I'm thinking of buying some!"

Bitcoin (like other cryptocurrencies) was originally designed to be a virtual e-currency that allowed the purchase of goods or services, using an electronic 'medium of exchange' not controlled by any government.

It could also be argued that it was designed to be a store of wealth, just like government-backed currencies.

However, since its invention, Bitcoin has been transformed into something other than an e-currency. It has transformed into a way to speculate.

A currency needs six key attributes to be successful:

1. Scarcity — supply is limited to maintain value.
2. Divisibility — $1, $2, $5, $10, $20, $50, $100.
3. Acceptability — will people take it as payment for a service or product?
4. Portability — you can put it in your pocket and take it with you.
5. Durability — it doesn't tear and pulp after getting wet.
6. Difficult to counterfeit — it's difficult to copy or make fake notes.

By having these attributes, a currency can evolve into a medium of exchange plus a store of value.

US dollars are a great example. In some developing countries, people use US dollars as legal tender rather than using their own country's currency.

US dollars are stable, readily accepted and backed by the government of the largest economy in the world. People recognise them, and will accept US dollars as a form of payment.

Bitcoin does okay on four of the six key currency attributes: scarcity, divisibility, portability and difficult to counterfeit.

However, storing cryptocurrencies can be problematic if data is corrupted, stolen or lost. There have been many cases of fraud and theft involving crypto traders.

People are also buying Bitcoin mainly to speculate. As a result, its value can fluctuate wildly from day to day, month to month or even year to year. It therefore cannot be used as a good store of value.

People don't want to spend their Bitcoins as money because they might go up in value after they have spent them. But at the same time, people don't want to save Bitcoins to buy a car or a house, as their value might go down.

Accepting payment with Bitcoin is also not common. As a medium of exchange to use to buy things, it is a long way behind normal currencies.

In May 2010, 1 Bitcoin was worth less than 1 US cent.

In November 2021, it reached over $64,000 USD.

Less than a year later, 1 Bitcoin was worth less than $20,000 USD[24].

Knowing that, would you save for a house with Bitcoin?

Bitcoin only goes up if people think it will, so they buy it. The only way it can go up is if more people are buying than selling.

When people's perception changes or governments ban or limit access to Bitcoin, then demand rapidly falls along with its value.

If you think the share market is a roller coaster ride, try cryptocurrencies!

Bitcoin and other cryptocurrencies, in general, are not investable assets. They are speculative only. Why? Because their value is driven by emotion, and irrational thought.

Bitcoin has no intrinsic value. It will never pay you a dividend or interest.

Nobody actually needs Bitcoin for anything — except maybe money laundering.

So, what do Bitcoin and other cryptocurrencies truly rely on?

The Greater Fool Theory.

The Greater Fool Theory

The Greater Fool Theory suggests that you can make money by purchasing an asset that is currently valued significantly higher than its intrinsic value, provided you can then sell that asset for a much higher price later on.

You are relying on a fool to come along, and buy your overpriced asset for more than you paid for it.

That 'bigger fool' is then hoping that an even 'greater fool' then comes along again and buys the asset for even more money than both you and the other fool paid for it.

Eventually, the price for the asset becomes so high that it is ridiculous to those with any level of common sense.

There are people out there who are completely aware that cryptocurrencies are worthless, but they have bought them knowing that there are plenty of fools who get sucked up by the hype. Fools who are driven by greed, and the thought of a quick win.

But once you run out of fools, someone is left 'holding the hot potato'.

And that person will be the biggest fool of them all.

If you bought Bitcoin in November 2021, and you still own Bitcoin, then you are the one with the hot potato. And you are someone else's fool!

Stay away from cryptocurrencies. Do not be a fool, big or small!

CHAPTER 4

Gearing (borrowing to invest)

When all you want is to be debt-free, the thought of borrowing more money can go against the grain.

Borrowing money to invest is not for everybody.

Debt complicates things and comes with extra risk.

Remember what debt is:

Debt is like fire — a great servant, but a horrible master.

I personally have borrowed to invest in property and shares, and profited from both.

How did I profit?

a) I acquired a large exposure to growth assets. Over time, they grew to be worth comfortably more than their initial debts.

b) The investments generate income (i.e., rent and dividends). I use this income to pay the interest on the loans and other expenses. And eventually the income I earn can be used to pay my debts down.

c) The dividend income from my shares is reinvested, and compounds the growth of my original investment.

d) Over the longer term not only has the value of my rental property investments grown, but also the rental income they produce. I am now comfortably, positively geared (i.e., my rental income exceeds all my rental property costs).

e) The interest on any loan used for investment purposes is a tax deduction, reducing the income tax I pay.

f) I receive other tax benefits from investing (i.e., franking credits from Australian company dividends, and depreciation from the investment property). More on this is explained later in this chapter.

I have exposure to growth assets I would otherwise not have, if I did not borrow money to invest. If the returns on these investments exceed the cost of finance, I become wealthier. And that is what has happened.

What are some key criteria I believe need to be fulfilled before you consider borrowing to invest?

a) **Good, stable working incomes**

If you are a full-time, permanent government employee in a role not impacted by economic downturns, and the chances of redundancy are low; then you have a good, stable working income.

If you are a casual fruit picker and your work is seasonal, this means if you get sick or injured (or there is no fruit to pick) you can't work, and will not get paid; then you do not have a stable working income.

A stable, regular working income is the most important criteria when borrowing to invest. Your salary income is the primary way you will service (pay) your debt.

b) **Emergency savings set aside**

This is essential. You must have savings set aside to draw on for an emergency. In doing so, you will avoid having to sell down an investment.

Your emergency savings will also cover the waiting period for an income protection claim, allowing you to continue to make your required loan repayments, and not default on any debt.

c) **Surplus cash flow (i.e., you spend less than you earn)**

If there is an emergency and you have dipped into your savings, then it is important to rebuild those savings to ensure that emergency savings are always on hand. You need to be a saver.

d) **A long-term investment time frame**
- 10 years or more for property.
- 7 years or more for shares.

Both shares and property go up and down in value (shares much more so). You must be investing over a time period that allows your investment to recover from a downturn and grow. This allows you to make sufficient profits to justify the risks you are taking on. And it ensures that when you eventually sell the investment, it is worth more than you paid for it.

Investing for the short- or medium-term using gearing, substantially increases the chance of a capital loss: where you sell your investment for less than you paid for it.

When it comes to property, you will spend around 3% of the value of the house in purchase costs (stamp duty and legal fees) just to buy it.

When selling the property, you will also easily spend another 3% of the sale price on costs (legal and real estate agent fees).

Thus, you need to make a profit on the sale of the house just to break even.

Property is not a short-term investment.

e) **Correct life stage**

If you are only a few years from retirement, then you shouldn't be borrowing to invest. Your primary source of income, and your primary way of servicing the investment loan is ceasing well before the loan could be repaid.

Your time frame is also too short to allow for the investment to recover, should it fall in value.

Gearing is a long-term wealth creation strategy, and should not be undertaken when wealth protection and preservation are more of a priority for you.

If you are over 55 and are still gearing, then you should have your exit strategy from your gearing position nailed.

You should know exactly how and when your gearing strategy will be wound up, and how you will move to a debt-free position.

f) **Adequate personal insurance**

Things happen. People are involved in car accidents, get cancer, or decide to bungee jump while on holiday in Africa. If you cannot work or you die, then your family's ability to service your investment loan disappears too.

What should be a sound wealth creation strategy can come crashing down like a house of cards.

Personal insurance is a financial safety net. It will 'catch' you and your family, and keep you on the 'straight and narrow' financially.

Without adequate personal insurance, the risks of gearing are too great to justify.

g) **An understanding of the risks of borrowing to invest**

It is important that you understand the investment risks

involved. For example, you need to be prepared for any falls in the share market. You cannot let yourself go into sheer panic if another GFC occurs, and the share market dives.

In fact, for the astute, this is exactly when you buy: remember the car dealership sale analogy, explained in Chapter 3?

Having a clear understanding of the risks involved in gearing, and how it fits into your long-term wealth creation strategy, will keep you committed to the wealth-building process.

And by being aware of the risks, you can better manage the risks of borrowing to invest by maintaining your emergency fund; ensuring your personal insurance remains adequate, or recognizing when gearing is no longer suitable for you.

h) **A higher tax bracket**

While it is not essential to be on a higher tax bracket, borrowing to invest is more tax-effective if you are.

Negative gearing versus positive gearing

Negative gearing

When you are at a barbeque chatting to friends, or listening to a financial commentator on the news, the 'gearing' most people will be talking about is negative gearing.

Negative gearing is essentially investing and creating a negative cash flow. The investment is removing more cash out of your wallet than it is putting in.

In other words, when you add up your loan interest payments, council rates, property repairs, insurance and land tax, the cost of all of this is more than the rent you are receiving.

Why would you do this you might ask?

You are relying on the value of your investment (in this case, property) to go up. You are seeking profits from your capital gain over time that exceed your regular cash flow losses.

Aussies love negative gearing because most of their investment expenses are tax-deductible. These investors give the nasty, horrible taxman a little less at tax time, or even get a bit back as a tax refund instead.

Negative gearing relies on your salary income to cover your cash flow shortfall.

If you lose your job/get made redundant, you are falling back on your savings for your investment loan repayments until you can get another job.

And if you run out of savings in the meantime, you are in trouble.

Positive gearing

Positive gearing is where your investment income from rent or dividends is higher than the cost of running your investment: loan interest, rates, insurance, repairs etc.

In this case, you are not relying on your salary income to support the gearing strategy. The investment, in effect, pays for itself.

Positive gearing does not necessarily mean that your taxable income — and therefore tax liability — will go up.

If you have borrowed to invest in a property, you may be able to claim depreciation of the building as well as other expenses as a tax deduction.

You can depreciate 2.5% of the value of the building (not the land value) every year for the first 40 years the building has existed.

If you spend more money on the building to renovate or improve it, you may be able to also claim this as a tax-deductible expense. It is important to speak to your accountant about how to do this.

If you have borrowed to buy shares in a company or a managed fund, you may receive franking credits to help offset any income tax liability.

Question: So why do Aussies prefer negative gearing?

Answer: Because they don't like paying tax.

The problem is, negative gearing is more risky than positive gearing: there is more reliance on your salary income to service the investment debt.

I have always been comfortable with borrowing to invest. While debt comes with risk and obligation, ownership of an asset that produces both income and capital growth provides an opportunity to build wealth that you wouldn't otherwise have if you didn't borrow to invest.

I have never been comfortable with negative gearing.

I have only ever used positive gearing as an investment strategy. I have never borrowed to invest unless the cash flow from the investment completely covers all of the expenses associated with it plus a small margin.

This can be quite restrictive when investing using borrowed money.

It also requires patience, as I can only buy shares or property that I like at a reasonable price. I don't change my parameters;

I just wait for the right time to buy.

This is my personal choice and my way of managing risk.

You may feel different.

Margin lending

Margin lending is borrowing money to invest in shares or listed managed funds.

You use the shares you already have as security for a loan, in order to buy more shares.

You do not use your own home or any residential property as security.

The bank will lend you up to a certain amount to buy shares, or invest in managed funds. This amount will depend on the type of shares or funds you are buying, and the value of the shares you have provided as security.

This is called the loan to value ratio.

The bank protects themselves by ensuring that the security for the loan is sufficient to clear the loan in full, in case you default and cannot pay the loan back.

If the value of your shares falls considerably, then the security protecting the bank's loan has also fallen. The bank may want you to stump up more cash, or more shares or managed fund units as security to protect their position.

This is what's known as 'a margin call'.

If you cannot provide the bank with more cash or shares after a margin call, they will force you to sell your shares at the worst possible time: when the market has fallen.

You are likely to suffer a loss.

The interest rate charged by banks for margin lending is higher than other forms of borrowing.

If you use your own home or other residential property as security for a loan, the interest rate you are charged is less than that for a margin loan.

But there is another reason margin lending is risky.

To help explain why, let's look at a hypothetical example of margin lending for an investment property (Note: You cannot use a margin loan to buy an investment property, this is just to demonstrate a key point).

Imagine you borrow $650,000 to cover the entire property purchase price of $625,000, plus your purchase costs of $25,000 (stamp duty, conveyancing fees, etc). You use both your own home, as well as the investment property, as security for the loan.

12 months later, the bank sends you a letter telling you that the properties in your area (both the investment property and your own home) are of poorer quality than they were previously because the property market has changed. Note: this does not mean they have gone down in value.

The bank doesn't want to lend you as much and demands that you pay back at least $100,000 to lower their loan exposure.

Come again?

You would have to find an additional $100,000, or sell the investment property (or maybe even your own home) to keep the bank happy.

You're kidding?

No!

In this case, the value of the properties you have invested in, have not necessarily gone down in value. The margin lender or bank has just decided they don't like the properties as much as before, and will only lend you less than before.

The problem?

You've already borrowed the money.

To apply the above case to real life, this is what a margin lender can do with the shares that you provide as security for a margin loan.

They can just decide that the shares you have provided as security for your loan are no longer as attractive to them. They may then demand a payment of cash or more shares as security, to cover their loan exposure.

To summarise why you should avoid margin lending:

1. It is an expensive way to borrow to invest.
2. It is a complicated loan, and difficult to understand.
3. It exposes you to a potential margin call, should the value of your shares or managed funds (used as security for the loan), go down in value.
4. It exposes you to the risk the bank will want some of their loan back at any time, not because your investment has gone down in value, but because they have changed their minds about how much money they are willing lend you, given the security you are providing.

This is why I have never taken out a margin loan — and never will.

Don't borrow to invest using a margin loan!

CHAPTER 5

Trade-offs

Paying off your mortgage faster versus contributing more to super

This must be one of the most common questions ever asked.

To clarify, the contributions I am talking about here are pre-tax (concessional) contributions to super. Not after tax (non-concessional) contributions to super.

First Question: Will you be worse off if you pay extra into your home loan?

No!

Second Question: Will you be worse off if you make additional contributions to your super?

No!

One of the most important things when setting goals is to consider what is most important to you.

For some of us, the thought of being mortgage-free is exhilarating, even more so than having a larger super balance. For others, the thought of saving enough to retire is more important.

Your level of motivation to achieve a goal is as important as the goal itself.

The average marginal tax rate for a worker in Australia is 34.5% (including the 2% Medicare levy).[25]

The tax on concessional contributions to super is 15%.[26]

By salary sacrificing into super, you have reduced your net income tax liability and in doing so made a 19.5% profit. And you haven't even invested your contribution into super yet!

Your savings held in super will also grow in a tax-effective environment, paying no more than 15% tax on any profits.

However, if you make extra repayments to your home loan, you will pay off your loan faster, saving you interest and taking years off your loan.

Should your marginal tax rate be higher than 34.5% (including Medicare), then salary sacrificing more into super becomes even more compelling than making extra home loan repayments.

But to answer this question objectively and not subjectively, we need to look at the mathematics.

Crunching the numbers scenario

A 30-year-old man on a $90,000 salary with a $500,000 mortgage at 4% interest over a term of 25 years is deciding whether to salary sacrifice $250 per fortnight into super, or put the $250 per fortnight into his home loan.

According to the AMP Rapid Pay Mortgage Calculator, if he made additional repayments of $250 per fortnight on top of his normal $1,319 fortnightly repayments, he would clear his mortgage in 16 years and 10 months. He would be mortgage-free before the age of 48 and save $62,438 in interest.[27]

THE SEVEN WINNING NUMBERS

According to the ASIC Moneysmart Super Calculator, by salary sacrificing an additional $250 per fortnight into super instead, he would have an additional $124,310 in his super fund by age 48.[28]

In addition to this, he would reduce his tax liability by $48.75 per fortnight or $1,267.50 per annum. By age 48, this would amount to a tax saving of around $22,815.

As you can see, making additional contributions to super rather than your home loan easily wins. Why?

For two reasons:

1. Because the rate of return on your super savings is likely to be materially higher than the interest rate you pay on your home loan

2. There are government tax incentives to both contribute to super and invest via super.

Original question: Do I pay off the mortgage faster or contribute more to super?

Answer: Do both.

While salary sacrificing more into your super wins mathematically, you are strengthening your financial position and building a safety buffer by being ahead on your home loan repayments.

Make the extra 5% contribution to super.

Apply the Winning Numbers 4 and 10 to your home loan.

I encourage you to use the ASIC Moneysmart calculator yourself, and run through several scenarios relevant to your financial situation.

Paying off the home loan faster versus investing outside of super

This is also one of the most common questions asked, and it relates very much to applying the Winning Number 20 to your financial situation.

For many people, paying their home loan off faster is more important to them than investing outside of super, in order to build another source of wealth.

This is because debt can cause increased stress and anxiety. And for some people, investing outside of super is outside of their comfort zone.

According to the rules set out in *The Seven Winning Numbers*, every single dollar set aside by you for the Winning Number 20 should go toward something that improves your financial position: initially clearing bad debt, saving for an emergency, investing outside super and/or clearing your mortgage.

What do I do myself? Both!

I have set a date where I want to be debt-free but also have enough saved (and invested) for retirement: both dates are before I turn 60. I have implemented strategies simultaneously to make sure I achieve both goals.

I have sat down and done the calculations. I know how much extra I need to pay into my home loan to clear my mortgage well before I want to retire. I have also done the calculations on what I want to have saved by the time I plan to retire. Given this will be before I turn 60 (the minimum age that you can normally access your super in Australia), I invest both inside and outside of super.

I haven't just focused on paying down my home loan in isolation, thinking that once the home loan is paid off, I can use the extra free cash flow to then invest. Why?

While I get a 'feel good factor' by being ahead on my home loan repayments, I also know that the compounding effect on my investments takes time to produce the results I want.

Your financial circumstances will be different to mine, so you need to consider your own financial situation and goals.

What are your key considerations when it comes to investing outside of super versus paying off your home loan faster?

1. When do you plan to retire: before the age of 60 or after?
2. Your age and life stage. How many years away from retirement are you?
3. What sort of investor are you: a more conservative investor or a risk taker?
4. Current interest rates: are they high or low?

If your goal is to retire before age 60, then you will need to save and invest outside of super to ensure you have sufficient funds set aside that you can access.

You will need to allocate part of the 20% of your wage (that we talked about earlier in Chapter 2 for the Winning Number 20) to an investment outside of super and grow it.

If you know you won't retire until after age 60, then just focusing on your home loan (and saving via super) may be the correct choice, especially if interest rates are high.

You can apply Winning Numbers 4 and 10 directly to your home loan, and allocate 20% of your wage to your offset account (as we also talked about with Winning Number 20 in Chapter 2).

For example, if you are 35 years of age and 20 years from your planned retirement age, your investment time frame allows you to take on sufficient investment risk to achieve a higher investment return after tax. It also allows sufficient time for the compounding effect to build your wealth.

Your expected return needs to be higher than the interest rate you will pay on your home loan. If you invest in a simple share index fund or other growth assets, then the chances are that you will achieve a higher return over the long term.

Ask yourself:

- Are you willing to take on sufficient investment risk, and withstand the ups and downs in the share market?

- Are you a 'nervous nelly' or a growth investor seeking a higher return?

If you are more conservative in nature, then the return you can expect from investing may be below the interest you are charged on your home loan. If this is the case, you may be better off financially to focus solely on your home loan.

For example, if you expect to get a 5% return on your investment and interest rates on home lending are 5%, then focusing on your home is preferable.

Why?

Because investing comes with risk and taxes, but paying extra into your home loan produces a guaranteed result, and there are no tax implications.

Remember there is nothing stopping you (if you consider yourself to be a more conservative investor) retaining a larger proportion of your 20% savings in your offset account and allocating a smaller proportion to an investment.

Consider your financial position, age and life stage, the type of investor you are, and the goals you have set for yourself.

Even after reading this chapter, if you are truly unsure and do not know what to do with the savings you are accumulating in your offset account, then I have a saying that I think is appropriate here:

If in doubt, pay debt out.

CHAPTER 6

Estate planning

The law is a complicated beast. Even lawyers grapple with it given how laws can be ambiguous, and therefore open to interpretation.

Quite often, it's down to a judge to interpret the law, and work out what it actually means.

Estate planning is legally arranging your affairs, to ensure your chosen loved ones receive your death benefits when you pass away, or become responsible for managing your affairs if you are incapacitated.

There are three key estate-planning areas I want to cover:

1. Wills.
2. Enduring Powers of Attorney.
3. Beneficiary Nominations.

Before I do, let's talk about estate versus non-estate assets.

An estate asset is an asset you can distribute via your will.

Examples of estate assets would be:

- Cash savings in a bank account in your name only.
- Residential property you own in your name only, or as tenants in common with other people. (Tenants in common have separate divisible shares in a property).

- A vintage car in your name only.
- A share portfolio in your own name only.

Non-estate assets cannot be distributed via your will but are automatically inherited by survivorship, or according to a set of rules.

Examples of non-estate assets would be:

- superannuation (by default)
- residential property held as joint tenants with someone else: Joint tenants do not have separate divisible shares in a property. If one person dies, the other owner/s inherit the deceased's share by the legal right of 'survivorship'
- insurance bonds (Investment bonds) where a beneficiary has been nominated
- life insurance policy where a beneficiary has been nominated
- a bank account held in joint names.

When it comes to estate planning, you will need to first determine what your financial assets are, and categorise them into estate and non-estate assets.

Your key estate planning areas

1. Drawing up a will

A will is a legal document that details how your estate assets are to be distributed upon your death. It will specify which assets are to be distributed, and to whom they will be given. It will also nominate who will look after your children (if they are orphaned, or you have lost legal capacity) and outline if you want to set up a trust for them.

Do not die without having an up-to-date will in place.

If you die without a will, the laws of the state you reside in will decide who gets your money. You may not like that outcome, if someone you do not care about inherits your wealth.

Take control now with a will.

If you do not have a will (or an up-to-date one), make an appointment to see a solicitor to have your will drawn up (or updated).

Don't write a will yourself to save money. It's not worth it. See a solicitor and pay them to draw up (or update) your will properly.

Before you go to see your solicitor, think about the following:

- Who do you want to have as the executor of your will? An executor makes sure that all your assets are distributed to the relevant beneficiaries nominated in your will. Your executor needs to be someone you can trust. Preferably around your age or younger to reduce the risk that your executor dies before you.

- If you have children, choose a guardian (or guardians) for them. A guardian is a person who raises children if both parents die or are incapacitated. Name your guardian/s in your will, and discuss your wishes for your children's upbringing with them when you do.

- Think about how you want your wealth managed after you die, on behalf of your children. Your children will need this to happen until they are ready to manage their own affairs. You can establish a testamentary trust via your will. A testamentary trust is simply a trust fund created when you die. (That's where the term 'Last Will and Testament' comes from). Your will document becomes the trust deed.

- Name a trustee to manage your testamentary trust. The trust will hold your wealth until your children reach an age you are satisfied is an age of responsibility. 30-year-olds make different life decisions compared to teenagers (mostly). Consider if the children's guardian/s should also be the trustee/s.

- Consider who might want to challenge your will. For example, have you been divorced and remarried? Do you have estranged former partners, or estranged stepchildren from your previous relationships? Have you favoured one child over another because you have a child who is a gambling addict, or a drug addict?

Eligible people can challenge your will, and sometimes have a court overrule your wishes. Discussing any potential issues with your solicitor, to ensure your will is drawn up to combat any possible challenges, is important.

It is interesting to note that only estate assets are affected by a challenge to a will. If you believe any people will challenge your will, a potential workaround strategy is to make an asset a non-estate asset.

I have known clients who have added a child onto the title of their own home as joint tenants. When the parents die of old age, the child included on the property title inherits the property by survivorship. The remaining children do not have the ability to take ownership of the home by challenging the will.

This strategy can cause family breakdowns, but it can be appropriate in certain circumstances. For example, if their house is the parents' primary asset, then they can prevent a child (who may be a drug addict) from accessing the house, selling it and spending the proceeds on drugs, by making another of their children a joint tenant on the home before they die. The only negative is that the parents may have to pay stamp duty on the title transfer.

2. Enduring power of attorney form

This is a form you complete to nominate someone you trust, to manage your affairs if you lose your mental capacity. An enduring power of attorney is a role with great responsibility. Your parents should each have one, and so should you and your spouse.

Just because you may be married to someone, doesn't mean they can gain access to your bank account in an emergency if the account is just in your name (and vice versa).

If your partner (or parent) is incapacitated in hospital, and you need to make financial decisions on their behalf, you will need an executed enduring power of attorney form to provide you with the necessary legal authority.

Each state should have an enduring power of attorney template form to download online.

But once again, speak to your solicitor about your power of attorney, when you have your will drawn up (or updated).

3. Death benefit nominations for your superannuation

Your superannuation is not normally dealt with via your will because, by default, it is not an estate asset.

Superannuation is dealt with according to the super fund trust deed: the trustees will decide who should receive your death benefit, and follow a process laid out in the trust deed.

You can choose a beneficiary yourself and legally bind the trustees to follow your instructions, but you must complete your super fund's death benefit binding nomination form. You will be able to download this form from your super fund's website.

Only certain people can be nominated as a binding beneficiary: your spouse, your child or a legal dependent. You can instruct the super fund trustees to pay your death benefit to any (or all) of them.

Not everyone is eligible to be a binding beneficiary. For example, you can't have an old friend from school as your binding beneficiary. If you do want your friend to receive a benefit, you may be better to nominate the executor of your will to be your binding beneficiary of your super. Your executor can then distribute your super death benefit to your old school friend as per your wishes.

This strategy converts your super from a non-estate asset to an estate asset. But it also exposes your super death benefit to any challenge to your will — so be warned.

Some super funds allow the binding nomination to remain in place until you die, while other super fund providers only allow the nomination to be valid for three years before it must be renewed.

4. Life insurance beneficiary nominations

When I was in the military, my whole unit was instructed to go to the lecture hall on camp. There was a sergeant from the Clerk's Office who gave us a presentation on our personal insurance options. We had special personal insurance provided to us, given that we were essentially uninsurable.

One of the lads had 'caught it up' on his last tour (this is Marines' jargon for "he died in combat"). He had a life policy and still had his estranged wife (who he had been separated from for some time) listed as the beneficiary.

He was in a new relationship, and his girlfriend was pregnant when he died. But because his estranged wife was still listed as the beneficiary, she received his life insurance payout. This was non-negotiable. His girlfriend never received any money. He had no children from his previous relationship with his estranged wife.

If you have a life insurance policy, ensure you nominate a beneficiary for your policy. The beneficiary can claim on the policy, and receive the proceeds discreetly if you die while the policy is in place. Furthermore, make sure you update the beneficiary nominated when required.

Life insurance benefit proceeds are not an estate asset, as long as you have nominated a beneficiary for your life policy. Any challenge to your will is irrelevant.

Estate planning is a complicated topic. You should talk to your solicitor for further estate planning advice, in relation to your specific situation.

My key estate planning points are:

1. Make sure you have a will, and that you keep it up-to-date.
2. If you have kids, choose a guardian — and include clauses to establish a testamentary trust for them via your will.
3. Complete an enduring power of attorney form.
4. Complete a death benefit binding nomination form for your super.
5. Complete a beneficiary nomination form for your life insurance policy.
6. Spend the money and pay a solicitor to advise you on estate planning.

 Always list where your assets are, who you bank with, what your account details are, and who your accountant/solicitor/licensed financial adviser is, on a sheet of paper. Then attach this piece of paper to your will (and store your will in a safe place). That way, the executor of your will isn't on a wild goose chase when you die.

CHAPTER 7

Insurance

Personal insurance

I had a meeting with a middle-aged couple while working as an adviser in a bank. It was a few years ago now.

I had never met them before, and the meeting wasn't going to involve me advising them.

They had contacted the bank seeking help. The husband had an industry super fund with some default personal insurance held inside his fund.

The bank I worked for owned the insurance company that provided the default personal insurance the husband had inside his super. And that was why they were in front of me that day.

The meeting was on a Saturday morning in the local bank branch. I had agreed to come in on Saturday given the urgency.

When they arrived, it was quite obvious that the husband was in a lot of pain. The extent of his pain meant his wife had to go back to the car park and get painkillers from their car during the meeting.

Essentially, he had been diagnosed with terminal cancer on the Wednesday of that week.

The sense of bewilderment they were experiencing was profound for me. It was quite clear they were still in shock. There was no emotion from either of them during the meeting, other than the husband's obvious pain.

I also found it unnerving that the husband was younger than me.

I reviewed his super statement, and looked at the insurance he had in his fund.

I noted the following:

- he had no idea what insurance he had in his super
- he didn't know what his super was invested in
- he had not completed a death benefit nomination form to ensure his wife received his super if he died.

But it turned out that he did have both life and total and permanent disability insurance.

It was quite clear that his life insurance policy held inside super, as well as his super savings, could be paid out early as a terminal illness payment. His diagnosis was that he only had six months left to live.

I ordered the required paperwork to be sent to them to make the claim. The following week I helped them complete the forms at a second meeting, and sent them back to the insurer.

I mentioned to them that his life insurance cover alone was enough to clear their mortgage in full. I just assumed that would be what they wanted to do.

But they decided not to do that just yet. In the time between appointments, their son and daughter had both taken unpaid leave from their jobs, and were coming home to stay. His wife quit her job. They were all going to be home to be with him until he passed away.

They were going to live off his early release terminal illness payout from his super fund, to allow this to happen.

I felt ashamed after the second meeting.

It is easy to focus on the financial side of things as an adviser. But when I saw them huddled together in the second meeting, I realised what was more important to them.

For their family, the next six months was time they would never have with their dad and husband again.

The home loan could wait.

They bunkered down as a family, nothing else mattered.

Your most valuable financial asset

If I were to ask you what your most valuable financial asset is, what would you say?

Would it be:
- your house?
- your 1958 FC Holden classic car?
- your home cinema system with Bose surround sound and subwoofer?

For some of us, it may very well be our unencumbered, multi-property residential investment portfolio. Well done to you!

But for most of us mere mortals, it is our ability to earn an income.

Think about it. You pay your home loan repayments, your living expenses and even other insurances with your income. Your whole financial position, and ability to build wealth, pivots around your ability to earn an income!

You may be living in a multi-million dollar house worth more than you will ever earn. But if you can't work, and the money stops coming into your bank account, you won't be living in it for long. Unless you plan to rent out rooms in order to pay the bills!

This is where personal insurance comes into play.

So, what is personal insurance about?

There are risks in life that we face every day. And there are financial consequences as a result of those risks. Should you not be able to work, suffer a serious injury or illness, you and your family may not able to pay your bills or your home loan repayments.

Further, should you or a family member become totally and permanently disabled or pass away, the outcome may be the loss of your home or even bankruptcy.

You can apply to an insurance company for protection for you and your family against the financial consequences of life's risks. In return, you pay the insurance company a premium (fee).

Insurance allows you and your family to be protected if something bad happens and you die, or you can't work due to an injury or you become critically ill.

There are four main types of personal insurance:
1. Life
2. Trauma (also called Critical Illness)
3. Total and Permanent Disability (TPD)
4. Income protection.

Let's look at each of these in more detail.

Life insurance

If you die, your chosen beneficiary receives a lump sum benefit payment, if you hold life insurance.

Furthermore, if you become terminally ill, your life insurance policy can be paid out early, and be used to take care of your family while you are still alive.

You can have life insurance in your own name outside of super, or it can be owned by and held within your super fund.

Trauma insurance

If you suffer a specific illness or injury such as cancer, a severe head injury, stroke or severe burns, then you will receive a lump sum payout to help with medical bills and/or rehabilitation if you have trauma insurance.

You can even use the proceeds to pay for things like ramp access to your front door for a wheelchair, should you become disabled.

When you claim on trauma or critical illness insurance, you do not have to prove that you cannot work. You only have to prove that you have suffered an insurable illness or injury.

You can only have trauma insurance in your own name. You cannot have it held inside your super fund.

Total and Permanent Disability (TPD)

This cover pays you a lump sum benefit payment if you suffer a severe illness or injury, and as a result, you can never again work in the job that you are trained and experienced to do.

After a certain waiting period (say three to six months), you will receive a TPD lump sum payout. The money can be used to clear your mortgage, and pay for medical bills, etc.

You can have TPD insurance in your own name outside of super, or held inside your super fund.

If you hold your TPD cover inside super and you claim it, you may very well pay tax on the payout: as a rule of thumb, plan to lose 22% of your TPD payout to the taxman.

Income protection

This insurance differs from the other three types of personal insurance. It is not a lump sum payment. It is a monthly benefit payment that you receive after a chosen waiting period (usually from 30 to 90 days or more).

The benefit amount can generally be up to 75% of your taxable income. You will continue to receive the benefit until you can go back to work.

If you never go back to work again due to serious illness or injury, the benefit can be paid for up to two years, five years, even up to age 65, or the age nominated on your policy.

You can have income protection cover in your own name, or held inside your super fund.

Income protection benefits are taxable, but the premiums are also tax-deductible if the policy is in your own name outside of your super fund.

Note: Income protection does not protect you against redundancy or dismissal. You can't just quit your job or get sacked and claim your income protection insurance.

So, which type of insurance do you need?

Well, if you're working, have dependents and a mortgage, you need all four types.

Each protects you in a different way.

Generally, it is better to hold insurance outside of super, where you as an individual own the policy.

If you hold personal insurance inside super, your super fund trustees own your policy (or policies).

Australia's superannuation laws can restrict the definitions of your insurance if you hold your cover inside your super fund, and therefore your ability to claim.

The reason why people hold insurance inside their super fund is convenience and affordability.

They may have personal insurance cover that's paid for and held inside their super because they really need the cover, and cannot afford to pay for it outside of super from their salary.

But it's important to remember that with every insurance premium dollar paid for from your super fund, there is at least a dollar less for your retirement.

For more information on holding insurance inside or outside of super, you should seek personal advice from a licensed financial planner based on your specific circumstances.

How much insurance do I need?

This is a very difficult question to answer, given each individual has different circumstances.

As a rule of thumb (and as a general guide only) you should at the very least have the following:

1. **Life cover** — enough to clear all your debt or 10 times your gross income, whichever is greater.
2. **TPD cover** — enough to clear all your debt or 10 times your gross income, whichever is greater.
3. **Trauma cover** — $100,000 minimum, enough to help pay for a large part of the cost of medical treatment.
4. **Income protection** — at least 70% of your gross income with a waiting period of 90 days, and a benefit period to age 65.

I have found that a waiting period of 90 days is the sweet spot.

A shorter waiting period of 30 or 60 days is more expensive. 90 days really cuts the cost down without extending the waiting period out too far.

Don't forget you need to have emergency savings to cover at least four months of all outgoings in your bank as a minimum. This will provide you with funds until your income protection payments commence.

Reviewing your personal insurance

As time goes on, you will pay your mortgage down and you will accumulate wealth. Your kids will grow up, fly the nest, and your net wealth overall will be higher.

Your ability to self-insure will increase, allowing you to reduce your personal insurance cover, as you get wealthier.

It is important to get your need for personal insurance down over time because as you get older, the cost of insurance cover increases.

Review your insurance needs in-depth between the ages of 40 and 45. If you believe you will need personal insurance after the age of 55, then you might want to consider switching your premiums from 'stepped' to 'level' premiums in your early forties.

Stepped insurance premiums go up with your age. They are initially cheaper than level premiums.

Level insurance premiums do not go up with your age, but they are a lot more expensive initially than stepped premiums.

If you reach age 55 and you're still on stepped premiums, you will experience huge premium increases every year from that point on.

All of this means you will need to compromise on the cost of insurance versus the level of insurance cover that you need.

Seek advice from a licensed financial adviser, if you are unsure what to do.

Applying for personal insurance

You have two options:
1. **The simple and easy way.**
2. **The more complicated (but better) way.**

Let's elaborate:

1. The simple and easy way:

    Apply through your superannuation fund for life and TPD insurance that amounts to at least 10 times your salary, or the total value of all your debt, whichever is higher.

    Apply for income protection insurance to cover at least 70% of your gross pre-tax salary with a 90-day waiting period, and a benefit period to age 65.

2. The more complicated but better way:

   Seek the advice of a licensed financial planner and complete a full needs analysis of your personal insurance requirements. Discuss the options you have available, and then apply for the personal insurance cover your adviser recommends that has been tailored to you.

The earlier you apply for personal insurance, the better.

If you wait until you are older before applying for personal insurance, any medical issues you have developed will hinder your ability to get cover. It may actually prevent you from getting some types of personal insurance at all.

If you have personal insurance cover in place when you are young, any subsequent injury or health issue you develop as you get older will not hamper your insurance claim.

A personal insurance policy is a contract. As long as you keep paying the insurance premiums, the insurer will honour the policy.

When you are young, bulletproof and haven't acquired any medical problems (obesity, diabetes, injuries to limbs, bad back, etc.), you are very easy to insure.

Take advantage of this!

Compromising on cost versus benefit

Personal insurance costs money.

Rarely can someone afford to be fully insured. You will need to compromise on the cost of insurance versus the benefits of having the insurance.

You will need to prioritise your different insurance needs, and insure what you cannot live without. Include your general insurance on your house, contents, car and pets in this thought process.

There is no point spending $4,000 a year insuring your vintage car collection when you have no personal insurance in place. Especially if you are working, have a mortgage, three kids, are a sole parent and you have no savings.

If you get seriously ill or injured and cannot work for a long period of time, you will be selling the vintage car collection.

Insure what is most financially important to you.

Even if that means you can no longer insure Gertrude your pet parrot!

Sorry Gertrude if you fall off your perch and break a leg, you're 'plucked'!

Health insurance

The Australian Government has taken a 'carrot and stick' approach to forcing a percentage of the population to take out health insurance.

The reason is simple. The public health system does not have the financial capacity to cater for everyone. There is not enough money allocated to fund healthcare costs in full, and as the population ages, this will only get worse.

The Australian Government therefore wants a certain percentage of the population to use the private health sector and not use the public health system.

More specifically, the Government wants people to use private health for such things as elective surgery (knee reconstructions, etc.) and childbirth.

In reality, health insurance forces the young and healthy to subsidise the sick and old.

Consider this:

- If you are in a car accident, you will just go to Accident and Emergency and be treated in the public sector.
- If you are pregnant, you can give birth in a public hospital.
- If you get cancer, you will be treated in the public health system.

For the young and healthy, there is little benefit in having private medical insurance.

What private health insurance gets you is to the front of the queue for elective surgery, or a private room after giving birth.

You can actually pay for this out of your own pocket. But for most people, it is too expensive, hence the need for private health insurance.

Health insurance comes in two parts:

1. Hospital cover
2. Extras cover — physiotherapy, dentist, dietitian, chiropractor, etc.

It is the Hospital bit that the Government is interested in.

Extras is just that, an extra bit added on by private health insurance companies for them to make money.

Extras cover has no bearing on the Medicare Levy Surcharge, or the Lifetime Health Cover Loading.[29]

So, what are the 'carrot and sticks' the Government has applied?

Carrot:

The Government will subsidise your private medical insurance premiums if you are on a lower income, but will gradually reduce this subsidy as you earn more.

Stick Number 1:

If your household earnings are over a certain amount, you will pay the **Medicare Levy Surcharge** if you do not have private medical insurance.

At the time of writing this book (the 2022/2023 financial year), if you as an individual earn over $90,000, or as a family earn over $180,000 per annum, and you do not have private medical insurance — you will pay the Medicare Levy Surcharge.[30]

The Medicare Levy Surcharge ranges from 1% up to 1.5% of your income. This is then added on top of the standard Medicare Levy everyone pays, which is 2%.

Stick Number 2:

If you do not apply for and get private medical insurance by the age of 31, the Government will apply a **Lifetime Cover Loading** onto your health insurance premiums later on in your life, should you apply.

The lifetime cover loading is an extra 2% added to your health insurance premiums, for every year you do not have health insurance over the age of 30.

For example, if you decide to take out private health insurance at age 50, you will pay an extra 40% (20 years x 2%) on your premiums every year for 10 years as a punishment.

Note: The cover loading penalty lasts 10 years before the government stops punishing you.

The wash up on health insurance:

- **If you're under 30 years of age, there is little value in health insurance.** Unless you have underlying health issues, or you believe you will need elective surgery on a regular basis, you will be better off saving up what you would normally pay in health insurance premiums and adding it to your savings/offset account instead.

- **You do not want to pay the Medicare Levy Surcharge.** If you earn an income that is over the Medicare Levy Surcharge threshold, you are better off to apply for basic hospital cover. When you get older you can upgrade your hospital cover in line with your needs.

- **You just want to have hospital cover, not extras.** Extras cover in most cases is a waste of money. Benefits are capped for each type of rebate, and also limited in terms of the overall claim amount per annum. You will most likely pay more in Extras cover premiums than you will get back when you claim. Add what you save (by not having Extras cover) to your savings plan, and leave the money in your savings/offset account instead.

Note: There is nothing stopping you reviewing your claims history with your health insurer and comparing this to what you pay in 'Extras' premiums. Most health insurers provide this information via their online portal where you can review the level of cover you have, the cost of this cover as well as your claims history.

Be aware, there are certain waiting periods for health insurance if you upgrade your level of cover. Plan ahead, and give yourself time to get through the waiting period.

For example: If you have decided to use the private health sector for childbirth, allow 12 months after you increase your health insurance cover, to be able to make a claim on pregnancy treatment and care.

General insurance and purchasing a car

If you ever go through the process of purchasing a car from a dealership, then it is an absolute certainty they will attempt to 'value-add' on several levels.

You will be offered all sorts of things, so the dealership can extract more money from you during the sale. Most of it is not good value for money at all.

But there is one 'add-on' that stands out in particular, in terms of not being value for money — and that is GAP (Guaranteed Asset Protection) insurance cover.

It is designed to cover the 'gap' between the insured value of your car, and what you may owe on it if you crash and write-off your vehicle.

It is not necessary. Focus on getting good quality, comprehensive car insurance that is suitable for your needs from a reputable insurer instead.

Never, ever buy insurance from a car dealership.

The dealership may actually not even mention GAP insurance and just add it to your purchase contract, especially if you have arranged finance through the dealership too. You will find you are actually borrowing money to pay for it.

Therefore, you are not only paying for GAP insurance you do not need, but you are also paying interest on money you borrowed to pay for it.

How do I know this happens? Because a car dealership did this to me! If I had not read through the paperwork, I would never have known the GAP insurance premium was there. It was added without my permission or discussion. And when I asked the finance guy what GAP Insurance was, he said it was just something they did! Is that so?

Arranging finance and insurance for the car elsewhere allows you to take your time, conduct your research and get the best deal for you.

It takes a lot of time to look at the small print and cost of insurance, and you will rarely be given sufficient time to consider the product being offered by a car dealership.

Avoid the high-pressure sales technique by simply stating that you have finance and insurance pre-arranged, thank you very much.

Car dealerships that sell you GAP insurance have a gap in their moral values.

The only thing you should buy from a car dealership is the car itself, nothing more.

CHAPTER 8

Being self-employed

Separating yourself from your business

One of the key issues I have noted over the years with self-employed clients (who may be operating as a sole trader, or have set up their own limited liability company) is that they do not financially separate themselves from their business.

It is common for self-employed people to not pay themselves a regular wage. They will do irregular drawings instead, particularly after they get paid for a big job. And they don't keep track of how much, and when, they draw funds.

Sometimes when I have asked, they don't even know how profitable their business is. They just leave it to the accountant to do all the paperwork: BAS statements, profit and loss and tax returns.

If you are self-employed, and not aware of how profitable your business is, then you cannot predict how much you can regularly draw as wages, and how much you need to leave in your business account as working capital to cover your business expenses.

By not paying yourself a regular fortnightly wage, you also take away your ability to manage your personal expenditure, and establish a regular savings and investment habit.

This has an often unnoticed — but profound — impact on your ability to build wealth, and ensure you are rewarded for your efforts.

You take on great commercial risk when you run your own business, and the buck stops with you.

That additional risk, stress, time and effort must be rewarded financially.

Separate yourself from your business financially. Start paying yourself a regular wage.

To enable this, you may have to build up additional working capital for your business that allows you to absorb any irregular payments from customers, and at the same time pay yourself a regular wage.

If this is what you need to do, then I urge you to do it. It may take some time to accumulate sufficient cash in your business bank account, but it will be worth it.

It is only once you do this that you can develop a wealth creation plan of your own.

Superannuation

I had a meeting once with an owner of a small local newspaper/magazine in regional NSW. His business model was to deliver his publication free to houses and local businesses, and generate income from advertising. Because his publication was free, its circulation was large enough to be attractive to an advertiser.

He was keen to get out of the business and retire. He was over 60 and tired. But when he came to sell his business, he struggled. He eventually found a buyer, but as part of the sale terms he had to continue to work in the business for another two years. Further, the sale price was nowhere near what he wanted or needed.

And why did he need a good price for his business? He had no super — at all.

So, what caught him out?

He was the business. If he retired, his clients would simply advertise elsewhere. For the business to be a going concern, he had to keep working at the newspaper/magazine to maintain the relationships with advertisers for the new owner.

The one thing he said which resonated with me, was that some of his longer-serving staff got more out of his business than he did, and they were all paid super. If he had a tough year, the only person who took a pay cut was him. And sometimes in really tough years, some of his employees were individually paid more than he was.

He did have his house paid off which was great. But he had very little to show for the 40 years of hard graft he had put in. He was destined to end up solely on the Age Pension.

You don't live life on the Age Pension — you merely exist. What you live with, is regret.

A majority of the self-employed people I have met over the years, do not make any contribution into super. Why? Because they don't have to!

When it comes to owning your own business, superannuation is even more important. Superannuation not only gives you the ability to save for retirement in a tax-effective environment, but it also gives you the ability to save in a protected trust structure.

This superannuation trust structure ring-fences your wealth from creditors and litigants, and is profoundly important for a business owner.

Once again, you bear commercial risk when you own your own business. It is a great benefit to be able to reward yourself for your hard work, by building wealth in an environment that is protected from commercial risk. Making contributions to super will enable you to one day have the retirement you deserve.

Do not rely on the sale of your business alone to fund your retirement.

Save for your retirement with super!

Self-managed super funds (SMSF) and your commercial premises

When I look at the offerings now from industry and retail superannuation funds, there is almost no reason why anyone should have a self-managed super fund.

Some industry super funds now allow you to buy and sell shares and build your own tailored share portfolio, making SMSFs even more obsolete.

When I look at the case for investing in residential property via an SMSF, I also observe the following:

1. Increased restrictions placed on SMSF lending.
2. Higher interest rates charged on SMSF lending.
3. Compliance requirements placed on SMSF trustees, who quite often do not know how to manage an SMSF.
4. Compliance, auditing and management costs for running an SMSF.

5. Tough penalties applied for breaching superannuation law.

The only justifiable reason I can see for having an SMSF is if you are a business owner, and you want to use your SMSF to fund the purchase of the commercial premises from which to operate your business over the long term.

If you want to do this, you buy your business premises with your SMSF funds. The business then makes regular rental payments to your SMSF at current commercial market rates. You use the rent to help pay down the debt incurred by your SMSF.

Why would a small business want to buy and own their commercial premises?

1. Because it allows you to secure a strategically important site that's essential to the ongoing success of your business. It prevents a landlord from potentially evicting you after your lease renewal terms expire.
2. Owning your business premises allows you to restructure your rental agreement in preparation for eventually selling your business to new owners. Being able to negotiate and placate any concerns a prospective buyer has for retaining access to business premises is a valuable negotiating tool, especially where the new owners may not want to buy the premises.
3. The rent the business pays may be high and equivalent (or close) to the principal and interest (P&I) loan repayments you would otherwise pay. After a number of years, you can own your business premises for little or no additional cost.
4. You can purchase and own your commercial premises via a separate legal entity (your SMSF) that's protected from any commercial risk: litigation or creditor claims.

5. If funding the purchase of the premises is otherwise problematic for you due to a lack of capital, you can gain access to your super savings in order to buy it.

6. The commercial property may also appreciate in value over time, adding to your retirement savings when you retire.

As you can see, buying your commercial premises is not just about providing you with financial benefits. It can also make strategic business sense.

A key consideration when it comes to deciding whether to buy your premises is your current lease.

If your lease states that your landlord is responsible for paying for water rates, insurance, repairs, maintaining and renovating your premises, then once you own it via your SMSF, it will be you that incurs those costs. This will negatively impact on the cash flow of your SMSF.

However, if your current lease states that you as a tenant are responsible for these outgoings, then buying the premises means there is no additional cost to your SMSF — you are already paying these costs from the business.

What are the risks of buying your commercial premises via an SMSF?

1. Managing the cash flow inside your SMSF will be paramount. If interest rates rise substantially, your SMSF may be burdened with P&I repayments not covered by the rent coming in. It may then be reliant on you making additional contributions to your super, to top up your SMSF cash flow.

2. Your commercial property may fall in value. This may be due to rezoning or development restrictions, or it may become flood prone.

3. You are risking your retirement savings to undergo this strategy. You are backing yourself and your abilities as a business owner. Only use this strategy if your business is in a good financial position, and you are good at what you do.

4. You are making your life more complicated by running your own superannuation fund. As a trustee, you have legal compliance obligations and the penalties for breaching them can be severe.

5. You will be heavily reliant on your accountant. Not only will you need to be good at what you do, so will your accountant.

It will be important to include your accountant in any calculations you do when deciding whether to buy your commercial premises via your SMSF. Your accountant can mathematically determine if this strategy is worth doing, based on your specific situation.

If you don't already have an SMSF and want to set one up to pursue this strategy, your accountant will also help you to establish it (along with your solicitor and financial adviser).

When it comes to purchasing commercial premises for your business, a Self-Managed Super Fund is not your only option. You can also buy your commercial premises via a trust fund or another legal entity established specifically for this purpose. There are several types of 'trust funds' that you can utilise, for example, a discretionary trust or a unit trust.

You may prefer this approach should you not want (or need) to use your superannuation savings.

Once again, seeking specialist advice from a licensed financial planner, your accountant and a solicitor will be necessary in this regard.

Finally, a discussion with your bank manager will also be important before spending time and money on establishing a SMSF or Family Trust. They will detail the lending criteria you must fulfill when borrowing money via an SMSF, and in comparison, via a trust. Consider how much you have available for a deposit and the loan term. You may want the loan term to tie in with your retirement plans, and when you want to sell the business.

Business expenses insurance

Business expenses insurance is an additional type of personal insurance to the ones discussed earlier, and it's designed for self-employed people.

It can help to keep your business running if you are unable to work due to illness or injury. Business expenses insurance should therefore be a serious consideration for any small business owner.

Generally, after a waiting period of 30 days, it will pay for your fixed costs for 1 year.

The fixed costs covered include:
- electricity, gas, hot water, phones
- rent
- leasing costs
- insurance premiums
- non-income producing staff salaries
- net costs of employing a locum (for doctors, dentists and veterinarians)
- security fees

Self-employed people generally have business expenses insurance alongside their income protection cover. This ensures that not only is their own income covered, but also their ongoing business costs while they cannot work.

For many businesses, the revenue generated by the principal/owner is paramount. Its loss is devastating to a business's ability to cover costs. Income protection cover in isolation may not be enough to protect you and your business financially.

Personal insurance can get very complicated for self-employed people, especially when you have business partners. It can be tied into partnership agreements and buy/sell agreements. Speaking to a licensed financial adviser who specialises in this area is crucial.

PART 3

Applying the Winning Numbers

It is impossible for me to write this book, and for it to seamlessly apply to your financial situation. There are millions of adult Australians at various stages of life, and all have different financial circumstances.

While comprehensive, the contents of this book are general in nature and require interpretation before application.

You will thus need to digest this book's contents, and consider how you will apply them to your specific situation.

If you are completely overwhelmed, then you need to seek professional advice from a licensed financial adviser.

However, if you would like some ideas on how to tailor *The Seven Winning Numbers* to your circumstances, then you may find the three scenarios I have written in this chapter helpful.

The scenarios are fictional as are the characters described in the scenarios. They demonstrate how people like you and me have read *The Seven Winning Numbers* and then applied the numbers to their own financial situation.

It is important to ensure that you apply *The Seven Winning Numbers* correctly. If you don't, you may end up not achieving the financial goals that are most important to you.

Let's look now at three scenarios where people have adapted and applied *The Seven Winning Numbers* to their financial situation and goals successfully.

SCENARIO 1

Young single adult

Two years ago, Aida (aged 24) decided to go to university to study physiotherapy. Her Mum was relieved. At 22, Aida appeared to have no direction, and was working as a casual in a retail outlet. She had finally got her teeth stuck into something, and would have a decent career ahead of her.

While studying, Aida worked in her dad's pool shop on weekends. Her Dad liked having her there, and Aida had proven to be better at the management side of things. Aida's dad didn't particularly like running a business, he just didn't want to work for someone else.

Over the Christmas break, Aida decided she would not go back to university to do her third year. She would instead take a break, and work full-time in the pool shop. Aida's dad would be going out on the road cleaning and servicing pools while she remained in the store. She decided that once she had established a good routine, she would go back to part-time study and finish off her degree.

Aida's mum was incensed. Her parents were divorced, and Aida's decision to manage the pool shop created friction between them. Her mum thought her father had pressured her to work in the pool shop full-time, but this was not the case.

Aida had thought about travelling, and even working overseas for a while. But over time she realised that running the pool shop was something that she was not only good at, but she enjoyed it. The variety of tasks was challenging but rewarding. Aida had to deal with customers, manage staff, stock levels, pool servicing schedules, and financial matters. She was organised and systematic in her approach. She also didn't take things personally: customers were customers.

Aida also liked running the numbers on revenue coming in, and expenses going out. There were customers who paid on account for the pool servicing, and customers who paid by card or cash when they bought pool equipment and chemicals in the shop. There were also outgoings such as rent for the shop premises, electricity, insurances, and two vehicles being leased and serviced.

Their accountant was involved with the business activity statements (BAS) and tax returns. Aida eventually became the accountant's go-to person when it came to discussing the financials. Her dad was happy with this.

She looked at what she was going to pay herself, and how her father only drew income from the business as dividends. He was now 49, and because he didn't pay himself a wage, he only had $78,000 in super. Aida had $6,500 in her super, as she had only worked casually after school before deciding to study physiotherapy.

Aida realised quite quickly that her dad would be working for a long time yet. The divorce had left him with a larger mortgage so he could pay Aida's mum her share of the house.

Aida decided that both her and her dad would be paid a salary plus superannuation. She paid herself $65,000 per annum plus 10.5% compulsory super. Her Dad supported this decision.

Aida had no savings. She lived with her Mum, and paid board of $200 per week. But she wasn't sure how much longer she would be living there, so she wanted to put some money behind her. Aida also wanted to start saving for a house.

Apart from running a car that her parents bought her, a mobile phone and board, she had no other fixed expenses. Every year Aida and her best friend went on a holiday together. They headed up to Port Douglas in winter when it was cooler and there were no box jellyfish in the water. This also worked well timing-wise, as winter is the quietest time of the year for the pool shop. She budgeted $5,000 for accommodation, flights and fun each year.

Aida had read *The Seven Winning Numbers* and realised how important it was not to waste the opportunity she had: she is 24 and has time on her side.

She decided she was going to save hard. She looked at properties to buy, and had set a target purchase price of $500,000 to get her on the property ladder. Aida wanted to save 25% of that amount ($125,000). That would allow her to put a 20% deposit down, plus pay stamp duty and other purchase costs.

Aida not only wanted to save a deposit for a house; she also wanted to save for an emergency, and if she eventually needed a new car, she wanted to be able to pay cash for it. Saving six months' worth of living expenses, as an emergency fund was not a lot, given she only had board, a mobile phone contract and a car to run. She didn't overspend on clothes or alcohol, and she was not materialistic.

Aida set another goal to save $15,000 as her emergency fund.

She looked at her after-tax income and living expenses, and how much she could realistically save.

After tax and Medicare, she cleared just over $52,108 per annum or $2,004 per fortnight.

Her fixed expenses are as follows:

FIXED OUTGOINGS	AMOUNT	FREQUENCY	ANNUAL AMOUNT
Board	$200	Weekly	$10,400
Car servicing	$650	Annually	$650
Car insurance	$2,200	Annually	$2,200
Mobile phone	$90	Monthly	$1,080
Holiday	$5,000	Annually	$5,000
Total annual fixed costs			$19,330
Total fortnightly fixed costs			$743.46

Before Aida started her savings plan, she thought about her super contributions and applying **Winning Number 5**. She was only contributing the compulsory 10.5% of her employee salary into super. So, she sent an email to their accountants to pay an additional 5% of her pre-tax (gross) salary into super when they processed the fortnightly payroll.

By doing so, she reduced her taxable income to $61,750 per annum. Her after-tax income also fell to $49,979 per annum or $1,922 per fortnight.

Aida already had one bank account open, so she opened two more bank accounts to apply **Winning Number 3**. She renamed her existing account her 'Everyday Account' and she named her two new accounts her 'Fixed Expenses Account' and her 'Savings Account'. Her fortnightly pay would continue to go into her Everyday Account every second Wednesday.

Aida then set up a direct debit for $850 to occur the Thursday after her fortnightly Wednesday payday. This $850 direct debit goes into her Fixed Expenses Account every fortnight. It covers her fixed bills and her holiday (that average $743.46 per fortnight). It also sets additional money aside each fortnight for unexpected expenses (such as new tyres for her car if she ever needs them).

Because Aida wants to save her $125,000 house deposit as quickly as possible, she decided to pretend she already had a mortgage. She added **Winning Numbers 20 and 10** together to help her save for her deposit faster. Aida then set up a direct debit for 30% of her after-tax wage to go from her Everyday Account to her Savings Account. The 30% direct debit amount she saves is $575 per fortnight (rounded).

After the direct debits into her Fixed Expenses and Savings Accounts, Aida is left with $497 per fortnight to pay for fuel, clothes, alcohol and going out with friends. It's pretty tight, but it's workable. Working full-time and studying part-time won't leave her with much spare time to splurge anyway.

It will take Aida one year to save just shy of $15,000: $575 x 26 = $14,950. Once she has achieved this, she will continue to build on it.

Aida spent some time researching investment products available to small investors. During this research, she reviewed the Vanguard investment fund options available, and decided on a fund that invests in global shares and bonds, not just Australian shares.

At the one-year point, she plans to also establish a regular investment plan, by investing in the Vanguard Diversified Growth Index (Exchange Traded) Fund. It has a Balanced asset allocation with 70% of funds invested in Australian and international shares, and 30% in bonds and fixed interest securities all around the world.

Aida prefers this diversification compared to just investing in Australian shares. Aida realises that she is not saving and investing for retirement, which is decades away. She is investing for a shorter time frame of 8 years or less. As such she doesn't want to have as many of the ups and downs that investing only in shares would bring.

Investing in the Vanguard Diversified Growth Fund is a necessity for Aida to reach her $125,000 house deposit goal sooner. Saving that amount would take over eight years at approximately $15,000 per annum. She needs to invest to make her savings money work harder for her.

She plans to reinvest any dividend distributions she receives, to boost her savings. Hopefully she will have $125,000 in less than 8 years as a result.

However, Aida does not plan to invest all of her savings. She will invest $2,500 per quarter (or $10,000 per annum) into her Vanguard Fund. The remainder ($4,950 per annum) will stay in her Savings Account to build her emergency funds.

So far, Aida has applied Winning Numbers 5, 3, 20 and 10, she has:

- arranged to salary sacrifice an additional **5%** of her pre-tax wage into super
- set up her **3** bank accounts, and
- is saving not just **20%**, but also an additional **10%** for her financial future.

Aida then looked at what assets her HostPlus super fund invests in. Her super funds were invested in Hostplus' default 'Balanced' investment option: 76% of those funds are invested in growth assets and 24% in defensive income assets.

Aida used **Winning Number 120** by applying the Rule of 120: she subtracted her age of 24 from 120 (i.e., 120 – 24 = 96). She then reviewed the HostPlus investment options available. She didn't want to build her own investment portfolio and have the worry of managing it, so she chose the 'Shares Plus' investment option for both her existing super and all future contributions.

The Shares Plus fund has 90% invested in growth assets and 10% in defensive income assets. This is much closer to her desired asset allocation of 96% than Hostplus' Balanced fund.

Aida understands that she is taking on more investment risk by having more invested in shares, property and infrastructure. But she also knows the expected returns will be higher. And given she can't touch her super for 36 years, she has time on her side to cope with the increased investment risk.

Aida has now used five of *The Seven Winning Numbers*.

The Winning Numbers of 4 and 55 are not relevant for her. She does not have a mortgage yet to apply Winning Number 4. And by using Winning Numbers 3, 10 and 20, hopefully the Number 55 will never become a problem.

Personal insurance and estate planning

Aida then looked at her personal insurance. She had default Life and TPD (Total and Permanent Disability) insurance provided by Hostplus Super. She saw that it was 'unitised' and had no idea what that meant, so she rang up Hostplus.

They explained that she was given several units of Life and TPD insurance and based on her age, a certain amount of insurance cover was provided per unit.

When she was older, the amount of cover per unit would fall every year. Aida didn't like the thought of that, and she also didn't think she needed life insurance anyway: She was single and had no dependents.

Aida noted that Hostplus allowed her to have TPD by itself (without having to combine it with life insurance) unlike most other super funds. This would save her money by not making her pay for insurance she did not need.

Aida also noted that she did not have any income protection insurance.

So, she applied to have her default unitised Life and TPD insurance replaced with the following:

1. Income protection covering 90% of her income with a waiting period of 90 days, and an eligible benefit period to age 65. Her income protection insurance will pay her 75% of her gross wage and the other 15% will go into Hostplus Super to keep building her super up for retirement.
2. Fixed value TPD insurance for $650,000.

Aida also went to a solicitor and had a will drawn up. She named her parents as equal beneficiaries and her uncle as the executor. Aida has no siblings.

She then completed a binding death benefit form for Hostplus and made her legal representative (her uncle, the executor of her estate) the binding beneficiary. This ensures that her super will go to her estate if she dies, and her uncle will then be able to distribute the benefits to her parents equally.

Aida's financial position now

Aida is really happy with what she has planned. She knows if something happens to her, she has insurance in place to protect her financially. Not only will she still be able to pay her bills, but her super will continue to grow too. And if she is not able to work again due to a total and permanent disability, she will have enough money to buy a house.

She also knows that she has all her fixed bills covered, and is saving hard to build up an emergency savings fund.

Once her emergency savings are in place, she will put her savings to good use and invest. This will grow her savings faster, so she will have the deposit she needs to buy a house sooner.

And even with her savings plan, she knows she can have a holiday every year with her best friend. She knows what she can afford to spend on having fun now without impacting her future plans.

Aida is taking advantage of being at home when the cost of living for her is low.

She is also taking advantage of one thing she has that her parents do not have — time.

SCENARIO 2

Young family

Sam (aged 35) is a self-employed electrician. He is married to Beth (32), who is a registered nurse. Together they have a son and a daughter: Tom (7) and Rachael (5).

Now that Rachael is in school, Beth has gone back to full-time work. They use after-school care and grandparents to help make this happen.

Beth kept her registration as a nurse going, while she was at home with the kids. This allowed her to keep her skills up-to-date, so she could get back into the workforce and progress her career.

Both Sam and Beth are relieved she is back in full-time work. She did not work at all while the kids were very young. As Rachael got older, she progressively increased her hours from one day a week, to three days a week.

While Beth was not working, they both went nowhere financially. It was a struggle to live off Sam's wage and social security payments alone (Family Tax Benefits).

Now, they want to get things going financially, and build their wealth. They have both read *The Seven Winning Numbers*, and are determined to use this new-found knowledge to set themselves up for the future.

Sam enjoys being an electrician and he doesn't mind being his own boss, but if he does not work there is no money coming in. He hasn't had a holiday that has lasted more than a week since he became self-employed five years ago.

Last year, Sam paid himself $106,000 from his business. He worked hard for that, putting in over 60 hours per week, every week. His main expenses are his truck (that he leases through his business), vehicle running costs, tools and materials. Sam draws money from his business whenever he has funds available.

He has not contributed any money to super since he became self-employed. Sam has his super with Australian Super from when he was an employee. It is invested in the 'Balanced' option and is now worth $32,000.

Sam actually considered getting a job in the mines, which would have paid $150,000 per year. It would have entailed being on a 'two weeks on, two weeks off' roster. The thought of working fewer hours a month for more money, and not having to worry about quarterly business activity statements, or chasing invoices sounded good.

But Beth did not want him to go away for two weeks at a time. After an argument over the issue, Sam has resigned himself to remaining self-employed. Being away for long periods of time would put too much pressure on Beth, now that she was back doing full-time work.

Beth is now on $74,000 per year. She did some research and found out that her employer (Queensland Health) offers a super contribution bonus: if she contributes an extra 5% into super, they boost their contribution from 10.5% of her salary to 12.75% at no extra cost. Beth's super is with QSuper and is worth $28,000.

Beth knows she is behind on her super savings, due to her time spent out of the workforce raising the kids.

Sam and Beth have an outstanding home loan balance of $407,000. The original loan was for $450,000 over a term of 30 years. Their house has gone up in value since they bought it, and is now worth $650,000. Their home loan repayments are $2,148 per month, with an interest rate of 4%.

Beth has a little hatchback car to get the kids to and from school, and to go to work five days a week. They took out a secured car loan for $24,000 with a 7-year term, and pay $392 per month. Beth and Sam still owe $19,000 for the car. The interest rate on the loan is 9.05% plus a monthly $5 fee.

They have $2,000 saved in their bank account.

Sam is happy to take risks when it comes to investing; he wants a high return on investment. He doesn't care about the risk; he thinks he has the time to make any loss back. If it means he can get rich and stop working, then he's keen. Sam doesn't have much experience with investing.

Beth is more cautious about money. She doesn't quite understand how it works when it comes to investing in shares or property.

They both decide that all they want financially is to have no debt, and enough to retire on. Beth is happy to work full time until she is 60 and then go part-time for another 5 years. Sam is not so sure about working, even to the age of 60. He saw his dad struggle with a bad back, and he had to stop working as a carpet layer at 52. His parents struggled financially as a result.

They take advantage of Beth's parents having Tom and Rachael for a long weekend, and spend the uninterrupted time sitting down with *The Seven Winning Numbers* to come up with a plan.

First, they decide to apply **Winning Number 3**. Beth and Sam go to their online banking and open up a new 'Fixed Expenses Account'. They rename their working account the 'Everyday Account' and their other account the 'Savings Account'.

Beth gets paid fortnightly on a Thursday. They look at when Sam draws money from his business account, and how often. Currently, he makes drawings whenever he needs money, and his accountant takes care of the rest.

They decide to change Sam's drawings to fortnightly, and for a lower total yearly amount than before. They agree that Sam can afford to pay himself $2,300 per fortnight while leaving sufficient funds in his business account to buffer against his business expenses in quiet months, as well as pay his taxes and super contributions.

Beth and Sam agree that Queensland Health's offer of boosting Beth's super contribution is an opportunity not to be missed. They decide to apply **Winning Number 5**. Beth sends her payroll department an email request to salary sacrifice an additional 5% into super.

She now knows that 17.75% of her pre-tax salary will be contributed to her QSuper Fund moving forward. Beth is very happy about this.

Sam emails his accountant and asks how he can make a contribution to super before paying tax. Being self-employed and not earning a fixed salary, he can't salary sacrifice.

His accountant advises him to open a new business bank account, and to set up a direct debit for $1,000 per month to go into this account from his main business account. Sam names the new account his 'Super Account' via Internet banking.

When he sits down with his accountant in May each year to look at his end of financial year tax plans, he will have money set aside to contribute to super.

Sam sets up a drawing of $2,300 per fortnight on the same Thursday that Beth gets paid. Beth estimates that after salary sacrificing 5% extra into super, her net take-home pay will be $2,138 per fortnight.

They now budget on $4,438 per fortnight as net take-home pay between them.

Beth applies **Winning Number 20** and arranges a direct debit of 20% of their take-home pay ($885 rounded) to be transferred from their Everyday Account to their Savings Account, on the Friday after they get paid each fortnight.

They then look at their fixed bills.

They are a bit taken aback at what they have to pay per month in insurances, loan repayments, rates, water, etc.

Beth sets up a direct debit for the Friday after they both get paid, for $2,400 per fortnight to go from their Everyday Account to their Fixed Expenses Account.

This leaves them with just over $1,150 a fortnight to buy their clothes, toiletries, alcohol, family trips out and have some fun. Beth thinks this is a pretty achievable budget, and that with commitment it will work.

They realise they have not considered a holiday in any of their expenses. But given Sam's work, they know that in reality a week's camping is all they could muster.

SCENARIO 2 — YOUNG FAMILY

FIXED OUTGOINGS	AMOUNT	FREQUENCY	ANNUAL AMOUNT
School expenses	$350	Quarterly	$1,400
Food	$250	Weekly	$13,000
Council rates	$800	Quarterly	$3,200
Water and sewerage	$220	Quarterly	$880
Car loan	$392	Monthly	$4,704
Home loan	$2,148	Monthly	$25,776
Electricity	$550	Quarterly	$2,200
Car servicing	$600	Annually	$600
Mobile phones	$150	Monthly	$1,800
Health insurance	$120	Fortnightly	$3,120
House insurance	$1,600	Annually	$1,600
Car insurance	$102	Monthly	$1,224
Total annual fixed costs			**$59,504**
Total fortnightly fixed costs			**$2,289**

Beth's parents will also chip in when the kids are on school holidays so Beth can stay at work. But they know this won't last forever.

So far, they have applied Winning Numbers 3, 5 and 20:

- They have 3 bank accounts to manage their money to ensure they are saving, paying their bills and still having fun.
- Beth is contributing an additional **5%** of her pre-tax salary into super.
- Sam has restarted his personal contributions into super by setting aside $1,000 per month.
- **20%** of their after-tax income is automatically going into their Savings Account in order to build an emergency fund. *This is particularly important given that Sam is self-employed and does not accrue any sick or holiday leave.*

They have four Winning Numbers to go.

They also want to apply **Winning Number 4** to pay their mortgage off faster, so Beth rings their bank. She asks them if they can have an offset account with their home loan. The bank says that they can.

Beth then asks how they can use their existing Savings Account as their offset account. The call centre person is very helpful, and emails them a form they need to complete, sign and return via online banking.

Once the form is received, it will be processed in seven working days, and their Savings Account will be linked and offset against their home loan.

Sam and Beth also look at their home loan repayments on their internet banking. They see they can change how often they make their home loan repayments. They decide to change from monthly to fortnightly repayments. They also change the bank account that the direct debit for their home loan repayment comes from, so it is debited from their new Fixed Expenses Account, rather than their Everyday Account.

Then they shop around to try and find better home loans with lower interest rates offered by other banks. In the end, they decide not to move banks and stay where they are, given that the 4% interest rate on their home loan is already competitive.

They are also happy to remain on the variable rate as it allows them to have the offset account attached, and to make extra repayments.

Sam and Beth then go to the AMP Rapid Pay Calculator[31] online and enter their home loan details. They took out a 30-year home loan five years ago when Sam was 30, and so they won't pay it off until he is 60 years of age (if they only make their scheduled repayments).

But they want to pay the home loan off by the time Sam is 55 (**Winning Number 55**) given that he is older than Beth.

They change the repayment frequency to fortnightly and see that their original home loan term drops from 30 years to 25 years and 10 months. They then play around with the online tool and add $200 per fortnight in extra repayments.

The result astounds them. By making normal repayments fortnightly plus extra home loan repayments, the original term of the loan drops from 30 years to 19 years and 9 months! With their offset account; the term should be even shorter.

They decide to try and find $200 every fortnight in extra savings by reducing their expenses. Although, they are worried that their budget is already tight, and aren't sure how they can do this.

They cannot find any way to reduce their fixed bills, and are also worried about having enough money to do things with the kids on the weekend. Sam loves going to the AFL, and the fun money in their Everyday Account will be important to them.

Sam and Beth also don't want to change their car insurance from comprehensive to a cheaper 'third-party, fire and theft only' policy because the car is security for their car loan. Doing that would be a big financial risk.

They decide to look at what they are going to do with the 20% they are saving every month. They come up with a plan that involves paying off their smaller debt first, and taking advantage of the 'domino effect' outlined in the **Winning Number 20** section of Chapter 2.

Out of the $885 that goes into their Savings Account (Offset account) every fortnight (i.e., approximately $1,917 per month), they will take $975 every month and put it into their car loan as an extra repayment.

They then went to the ASIC Moneysmart Personal Loan Calculator online. They worked out that if they add $975 per month to the existing $392 per month they already pay, then they would clear the remaining car loan balance in just 1 year and 3 months, rather than 5 years and 3 months, saving almost $4,000 in interest.

They will still be saving over $10,000 across the year in the Savings Account even when they make these extra car monthly loan repayments.

Once the car loan is paid out, they will free up 8% of their fixed expense costs. That's not quite 10% of total expenses (**Winning Number 10**), but it's a big improvement.

They will then allocate all of their former monthly car loan repayments or $392 per month ($181 per fortnight) as extra home loan repayments (as per **Winning Numbers 4 and 10**).

They will then continue to accumulate 20% of their net income as savings into their Savings/offset account until they have $30,000 or about 6 months' worth of living expenses sitting in there.

Once they achieve this goal, they will start an investment plan using some of the 20% in savings set aside every month: one quarter of what is saved will remain in and build the offset account balance, and three quarters will be invested.

Sam and Beth understand the benefits of investing outside of super, but they are tempered by the fact that Sam does not have the security that comes with being a full-time employee. Therefore, continuing to build their emergency savings is important.

They decide that once they reach $30,000 in savings, they will then invest 75% of their future savings into the Australian Foundation Investment Company (AFIC) in joint names. They will also set up an automatic dividend reinvestment back into more AFIC shares.

Beth's uncle suggested this to them, as he had invested in AFIC for over 40 years. He explained that it is a listed investment company that would make all the investment decisions for them, it has a good track record, low fees and it's diversified.

The remaining quarter of the 20% they are saving, will remain in their Savings Account, and continue to build their existing emergency funds, offset against their home loan.

In a number of years' time their savings will be a lot more than six months' worth of living expenses. And when Beth needs a new car in the future, maybe they can use some of the savings to buy it, rather than borrowing the whole amount like they did last time.

Next, Sam and Beth want to apply **Winning Number 120**. They log onto their super fund websites to see their current investment options. Sam is in the 'Balanced Investment' option with Australian Super. He sees that Australian Super will allow him to put his own portfolio together, and even buy and sell his own shares. They also have several pre-mixed (all in one) investment options that would do all the investing for him, so he wouldn't have to worry about it.

Sam uses the Rule of 120 to help him make his investment decision. He subtracts his age (35) from 120 and comes up with an 85% investment in growth assets as his ideal scenario. He notes that the Australian Super Balanced option is 80% invested in growth assets, but that the Australian Super High Growth option is 93% invested in growth assets.

Sam considered buying shares in his super and doing his own investing, but after some thought he realised that he did not know enough, and will leave it to the fund manager to make these decisions.

Sam then decides to switch his super to the High Growth Option. While he understands this decision comes with more risk, he wants a higher return and is prepared to take that extra risk. Sam also understands he can withstand the ups and downs given his investment time frame — he cannot touch his super for at least another 25 years until he is 60 and retired.

Beth uses the calculator on her phone, and subtracts her age (32) from 120. She ends up with an 88% investment in growth assets as her ideal scenario.

She is currently invested in the 'Lifetime Outlook' option in her super fund (QSuper). Beth reads that this fund is more aggressive when she is younger, but automatically becomes more conservative as she gets older. She really likes that approach.

Her current investment allocation in the fund at her age is 87% in growth assets and 13% in defensive income assets. That's pretty close to what she should have, using the Rule of 120. So, she keeps the investment option she already has in her super fund.

Sam and Beth have now applied Winning Numbers 4, 55, 10 and 120:

- They have gone through all 4 ways to pay their home loan off faster so they can pay off their home loan before Sam is 55.

- They have attempted to find an extra **10%** of savings each month by aggressively targeting their car loan with extra repayments. Once their car loan is paid out, their fixed expenses will reduce.
- They have used the **Rule of 120** to work out the ideal investment strategy for their super funds.

Personal insurance and estate planning

Next, Sam and Beth look at their personal insurance. They both have the default life and TPD cover inside their super. Neither of them has income protection or trauma insurance. They toy with the idea of seeing an adviser, but decide not to.

Because they feel their budget is tight, they decide to pay for additional insurance cover inside their super. They understand this will mean less money for their retirement, as their super funds will be using some of their contributions to pay the insurance premiums.

They both apply via their super funds for ten times their salary for life and TPD cover, as well as income protection covering 75% of their incomes, with a 90-day waiting period and benefits to age 65.

Sam and Beth then make an appointment to see a solicitor. They want Beth's sister to be the guardian for Tom and Rachael if something happens. They also want to make her the trustee of any money left to the kids. Sam and Beth decide to make Beth's sister and husband the joint executors of their will.

Sam and Beth have each other as their preferred beneficiaries for their super funds. They think this is OK, but Beth rings QSuper and finds out that a preferred beneficiary is not a binding on her superannuation fund.

The QSuper call centre operator directs Beth to the Binding Nomination Form on the QSuper website. Beth prints this off, and Sam does the same for his Australian Super fund. They complete the forms, and get their neighbours to witness their respective signatures.

Going through their finances has been an exhausting process for Sam and Beth. But they now feel in control of their financial futures.

They are also happy knowing they will be mortgage-free, have an investment fund (they can access before age 60) and a lot more in super by the time they are 55. And if something happens, they have personal insurance in place to help protect them financially. Not only that; their children will be taken care of.

Sam and Beth estimate that by applying The Seven Winning Numbers, they will achieve the following:

- **Car loan**
  Pay out their secured car loan 4 years early, saving almost $4,000 in interest.

- **Home loan**
  Pay out their home loan before Sam turns 55, saving over $80,000 in interest.

- **Beth's super**
  Based on her annual income ($74,000), a rate of return of 7.5%, salary sacrifice contributions of 5% and the additional employer super guarantee contributions, her balance will grow to be worth around $470,000 by the time she is 60.

- **Sam's super**
  Based on $12,000 annual contributions and a rate of return of 8.5%, his balance will be around $440,000 by the time he is 60.

- **Joint investment in the Australian Foundation Investment Company**
  Using an online compounding calculator, based on an initial $2,000 investment, quarterly purchase of shares worth in total $17,250 every year, average annual returns of 8.5% and the reinvesting of dividends, Beth and Sam believe they will have shares in AFIC worth over $550,000 by the time Sam turns 55.

Sam and Beth have set themselves up for a secure financial future. They are living within their means, and going without some of life's luxuries. But they will be debt-free by the time Sam is 55, and given the physicality of Sam's job, they will be able to afford for him to either stop working or significantly reduce his workload before he turns 60. They will also have enough saved for the retirement they deserve.

SCENARIO 3

Middle-aged couple with teenage children

Grant (aged 44) is an IT manager on a salary of $180,000 per year. Wendy (42) is a marketing executive on a salary of $175,000.

Grant has $217,500 in his super with the Australian Retirement Trust. Wendy has $181,200 with UniSuper. She stopped working for several years when they had children and as a result, her super balance is lower.

Grant and Wendy's home is worth $1.5 million, and they have a current outstanding balance on their mortgage of $698,000 @ 4.35% interest. Several years ago, they upsized to a larger house. The new mortgage was originally for 30 years and has another 26 years to run. Fortnightly repayments are $1,866.

Their children attend private school. Oliver, aged 17, is in Year 12, and Amelia, aged 15, is in Year 10. School fees for the children are $12,000 each for the year, plus other costs such as uniforms, camp, sport and excursions. Oliver has his learner driver's licence, and will be eligible to sit his driving licence test later in the year.

Private schooling for their children is important for Grant and Wendy. They want them to have the best start in life and believe a good education is key to that. They will also be pushing the children to go to university and get a degree, before taking any time off to travel etc.

When Oliver gets his driver's licence, they want to buy him a car so he can get out and about and have fun. They also have an ulterior motive, which is to relieve themselves of any taxi duties. When Amelia is able to drive, they want to buy her a car too.

They will be looking at second-hand cars worth $15,000 for each child.

Grant and Wendy have no savings, nor have they ever done a budget.

They each have a credit card account with total debt outstanding of around $14,000. Their combined credit card limits total $30,000.

They make their credit card payments on time, but do pay interest on the outstanding balance. This is because their credit cards are not paid in full within the interest-free period.

Grant and Wendy each have a car, but no car loans. In the past when they needed to buy a car, they just increased their home loan and drew on the equity they had built up. They weren't sure if this was the right thing to do, but the bank manager said this was the cheapest interest rate for any loan to buy a car.

They have the top Hospital and Extras cover for their family with BUPA Health Insurance.

Wendy developed breast cancer eight years ago. She went through a round of chemotherapy and radiotherapy in order to beat it. She also had part of her left breast removed, along with some lymph nodes under her left arm. Thankfully, the cancer has not come back since.

Wendy vividly remembers her breast cancer journey. She remembers first feeling the lump, and thinking it was impossible that it was cancerous because cancer was something *other people* got. She also remembers food tasting metallic while she was having chemo, along with the stares from people when her hair fell out.

For the first two years after her treatment ended, she went to her check-ups half expecting the cancer to return. But over time, her check-ups became less frequent, and her fear that the cancer would return waned.

But the impact it has had on Wendy, and how she lives her life, has not faded: she lives for the now, and relishes catching up with friends over lunch or a coffee.

Every year the family holidays at the Sunshine Coast: Christmas, for them, has to be at the beach.

Grant doesn't mind Wendy's 'live for now' approach to life. He thought he was going to lose her when she was first diagnosed. He has also worried about the cancer coming back ever since. When Wendy realised how much Grant dwelled on it, she forced herself to worry less, and also stopped showing it.

Grant and Wendy upgraded their house from a three to a four-bedroom property with a pool several years ago. The new home has plenty of space for the family plus a teenager's retreat for when their friends stay. Barbeques around the pool in summer are a regular.

Grant was recently given a copy of *The Seven Winning Numbers* by a friend, who thought he might find it an interesting read. He spent the next few weeks reading it in his spare time.

After he had finished the book, he started to think about when he wanted to retire. He enjoyed his job, and the thought of retirement (or planning for it) hadn't occurred to him before. It certainly had not occurred to Wendy. But he realised that they would have to retire someday. Age would eventually catch up with them.

Grant thought about what they were going to do with their mortgage. On paper, it had another 26 years to go. This would mean he would be 70 when they made their last repayment. He couldn't see himself working past 65. He also couldn't see Wendy working when he retired. So how were they going to be debt free in time for retirement?

Grant then thought about their super funds. Neither of them had ever thought about what assets their super funds were invested in before. He then wondered how much they would have saved in super by the time they did retire. Would it be enough?

Neither Grant nor Wendy had ever made any additional contributions to their super funds, nor had they chosen beneficiaries to receive their super benefits if they died.

Grant and Wendy also only had the default insurances in their super: life, TPD and income protection cover with a maximum benefit period of two years.

Neither of them had any trauma (critical illness) insurance. Grant didn't even know it existed. He was also a bit concerned that if he were in a car accident and couldn't work again, then two years of income protection payments wouldn't help much.

He also noticed that their life and TPD insurance cover amounts held inside super were falling in value every year and wondered why?

Wendy had claimed on her income protection cover when she had cancer. That income protection cover still remains in place.

Grant then thought about what would happen financially if something were to happen to either of them. They had a lot less debt when Wendy first got cancer, and they rely heavily on both of their incomes to pay their bills and mortgage repayments.

They had simply not discussed any of this before. He thought it was time for the two of them to talk about their financial future together.

They sat down together, and Grant started talking about *The Seven Winning Numbers*. He also talked about the following topics with Wendy:

1. When she wanted to retire.
2. When they wanted to be debt-free.
3. How they would pay the mortgage, school fees and living expenses if something happened to either of them.
4. How much money Wendy thought they would need in retirement.

Wendy actually felt scared talking about the next 30 to 40 years. She had been in remission for a while now and she didn't want to jinx herself.

Grant emphasised the importance of planning for their financial future, and that Wendy wouldn't be jinxing anything by doing it. If anything, making sure that there was no financial stress and worry in their lives would help keep her healthier. Wendy just nodded. Deep down she knew that this was a conversation they had been avoiding.

Wendy wanted to be able to retire early enough to still be able to go overseas on holidays. She hadn't done all the travelling she wanted to do before they had Oliver and Amelia, and she didn't want to retire only to find they were too old to travel.

Wendy also didn't want to keep working past 60. Grant would be 62 then. This was a bit earlier than he expected to retire.

Grant and Wendy then discussed what would have to happen for them to retire when Wendy reached age 60.

SCENARIO 3 – MIDDLE AGED COUPLE WITH TEENAGE CHILDREN

In reality, they would have to have paid their mortgage and saved enough to live off, as they would be way under the Age Pension age (67). And even then, neither of them wanted to scrimp and scrape on the Age Pension alone. After what they had been through, retirement needed to be something to look forward to.

If they were to go travelling, they would also need to save a lot. And if they were to retire well before the Age Pension age, they would have to accept that they would use up a lot of their superannuation by age 67, or choose to work part-time in between travelling and semi-retirement.

They both realised that they actually had no idea how they would afford this, or if these ages were achievable.

Grant and Wendy were both keen to know what they could do to take charge of their financial future. Grant gave Wendy *The Seven Winning Numbers* and over the next couple of weeks, she read it in full.

They then sat down together, and decided to go through each of **The Winning Numbers** one by one.

They only had one bank account, no savings and two separate credit cards. With a combined $14,000 on their credit cards, it was going to take a little while to clear their balances, and they were probably going to pay 20% interest on part of the balance.

Grant and Wendy decided to apply **Winning Number 3** and opened up two other bank accounts. They got in touch with the bank, and had one of those accounts linked to their home loan as an offset. They named the offset account their 'Savings Account'.

The other new account they named their 'Fixed Expenses Account' and they renamed their existing account to be their 'Everyday Account'.

They then sat down and worked out their fixed expense amounts.

Grant and Wendy had fixed commitments over a year that cost them an average of $5,912 per fortnight. They had budgeted a lot for a holiday because they knew, in all honesty, they splurged quite a bit when they were at the beach.

They then looked at what they were paid after tax; combined, they brought home just over $246,417 (rounded) per year (or $9,477 per fortnight).

FIXED OUTGOINGS	AMOUNT	FREQUENCY	ANNUAL AMOUNT
Private school fees	$6,000	Quarterly	$24,000
Additional school expenses	$1,100	Quarterly	$4,400
Groceries	$600	Weekly	$31,200
Council rates	$1,015	Quarterly	$4,060
Water and sewerage	$315	Quarterly	$1,260
Car loan	$nil	N/A	$nil
Home loan	$1,866	Fortnightly	$48,516
Electricity	$700	Quarterly	$2,800
Car servicing	$1,300	Annually	$1,300
Health insurance	$208	Fortnightly	$5,408
House and contents insurance	$4,000	Annually	$4,000
Mobile phone contracts x 4	$200	Monthly	$2,400
Internet and pay TV	$150	Monthly	$1,800
Car insurance	$215	Monthly	$2,580
Holiday	$20,000	Annually	$20,000
Total annual fixed costs			$153,724
Total fixed costs fortnightly			$5,912

Grant and Wendy both just looked at each other and thought, *where is the rest of the money going? What are we spending our money on?*

Neither of them could answer those questions.

First, they set up a direct debit for $6,200 per fortnight from their Everyday Account to their Fixed Expenses Account. They were happy to put in a little extra than they needed each month ($5,912) just in case some utilities (electricity, water) cost more than expected or a car needed repairs.

Wendy then applied **Winning Number 20** by doing a quick calculation of 20% of their take-home pay. She set up a second fortnightly direct debit for $1,900 (rounded) from their Everyday Account into their Savings Account.

Grant and Wendy realised they had a lot of existing direct debits going to their credit cards for reward points. They removed all of these. They then moved all the direct debits for their fixed expenses to their Fixed Expenses Account.

Any other direct debits that were not going to their Fixed Expenses Account, such as pay TV subscriptions, were now going to their Everyday Account. They decided that they would cancel Kayo and Netflix, and just have Foxtel.

They then looked at their credit cards. They decided they would cancel the card in Grant's name, once their combined credit card debt had been cleared. They would then apply for a second card for Grant on Wendy's credit card account, and reduce their credit limit to $4,000 to be shared between the two of them.

They also decided that the card would only be used for online purchases, or if their debit cards did not work in a buying situation. They still weren't sure if the credit card would cause them problems by allowing them to spend too much.

But they felt that by sharing one credit card account, and lowering the credit limit, their spending would be kept in check.

They took stock of what they would have available to spend, and what they would save every fortnight:

Everyday account	$1,377
Fixed expenses account	$6,200
Savings account	$1,900

Limiting discretionary spending to $1,377 per fortnight would take some discipline, especially with all four members of the household wanting to do things. Grant and Wendy realised they would need to sit the kids down and explain to them they couldn't just have what they wanted all the time.

Grant and Wendy then thought about how they were going to save for the kids' cars ($15,000 each). This money could not come out of their Savings Account, and they didn't want to draw from their home loan again either.

They decided to forgo the family holiday this coming Christmas and keep these funds in their Fixed Expenses Account instead. This $20,000 saving would cover the cost of Oliver's car and provide them with the first $5,000 to put towards Amelia's car. They would then reduce the budget for the annual family holiday down to $15,000 (from $20,000), freeing up another $5,000 per year to save for Amelia's car in the following two years.

Grant and Wendy would explain to the kids that not having a holiday this year would allow them to have a car each.

They didn't expect any resistance, given the freedom the cars would bring.

Once their credit card balances had been cleared, they decided they would build up their Savings Account to $55,000 before they would even look at investing. This amount would become their emergency fund. By the time they paid off the credit card and saved this amount, Amelia would not be far off finishing school. This would be the perfect time to review their finances again, and establish a new plan and start investing outside of super.

Grant and Wendy then looked at their super funds. They both felt they were behind in building their super savings, and decided to apply **Winning Number 5**.

They each spoke to their payroll departments at work, and started salary sacrificing an additional 5% into their super funds. The payroll department at Grant's work noticed that he couldn't contribute the full 5% into super because his employer is already contributing $18,900 as a superannuation guarantee contribution. Given the concessional cap into super is $27,500 per annum; Grant can only contribute another $8,600 per annum as a concessional contribution.

After salary sacrificing into super, Grant and Wendy saw a corresponding reduction in their take-home pay and were not sure what to do about their saving and spending budgets.

Given their take home pay had fallen by over $400 per fortnight, they decided to reduce the monthly direct debit to their savings account by $150 per fortnight to reflect the reduction in take home pay and make their savings plan more achievable:

Everyday account	$1,200
Fixed expenses account	$6,200
Savings account	$1,750

So far, Grant and Wendy had applied Winning Numbers 3, 20 and 5:

- They now have **3** bank accounts. This automates and forces them to save, ensures their fixed bills are covered, and positions them so that they know how much they can spend on having fun and non-essentials.
- They are saving roughly **20%** of their take-home pay, which they will use to clear their credit cards, and then build a savings fund for emergencies.
- When the kids get their driver's licences, they will have saved up enough money to pay cash for the cars. Just by forgoing a couple of weeks at the beach for their family holiday, the kids will have ridiculous amounts of freedom with their own wheels.
- They are also contributing in and around **5%** more to super, and in doing so, reducing their income tax as well as boosting their retirement savings at the same time.
- They are starting to live within their means and put their hard-earned incomes to better use. Those retirement plans they wanted are becoming more realistic!

Grant and Wendy then turn to their home loan. They look at the **Winning Numbers 4 and 10** and how to apply them.

Grant and Wendy got the AMP Rapid Pay Calculator[32] up on the computer and they entered their current loan details. They already paid their home loan fortnightly, and now had an offset account (*2 of the 4 Winning Number 4 strategies to pay off your home loan faster*). It was now down to finding extra savings in order to make extra loan repayments, plus finding a better home loan deal (*the other 2 Winning Number 4 strategies*).

Oliver would finish school in nine months, which would free up a minimum of $12,000 per year in school fees. Grant and Wendy both openly admitted to each other they would have just spent this money and not saved it.

They then looked at their health and general insurances: they didn't want to move away from top hospital cover given Wendy's medical history. They decided to cancel the extras cover and free up $60 per fortnight instead ($1,560 per year). They also shopped around for house and contents insurance, and found a cheaper, yet reputable, insurer. This saved another $450 per year.

Their combined savings on school fees and insurance freed up another $14,010 per year (or about $539 per fortnight) that they both knew should be allocated to their home loan as extra repayments — and not spent.

Next, they shopped around and looked for better home loan deals. They found a lender who offered a 4.05% variable rate with an offset account attached. They then went back to their current lender with their approval from their prospective lender, and asked if they could match the offer. Given their equity position and income, their existing bank matched the lower rate, saving them 0.30% interest.

They put both the lower interest rate, and extra home loan repayments ($539 per fortnight), into the calculator.

Based on their original loan amount and original loan term, the outcome was their home loan being paid off eight and a half years earlier, and they would save over $200,000 in interest!

Note: if you reduce your interest rate via refinancing, then the calculator will also reduce your standard fortnightly repayments. You can simply ignore this or slightly increase your extra repayments to compensate.

Furthermore, different online calculators will produce slightly different outcomes dependent on the assumptions made and formulas used.

So, what did they need to repay per fortnight, to achieve their goal of fully repaying their home loan before Grant turns 55 in 11 years?

According to the calculator, they would have to increase their additional fortnightly repayments from $539 to at least $1,300. This would be impossible until Amelia finished school.

Regardless, they decided to aim to find $20,000 in savings based on the Winning Number 10 (10%) to use as extra repayments on their home loan. They already had $14,010 from school fee and insurance savings, they just needed to find another $5,990.

Grant and Wendy looked at their mobile phone contracts, but they were both locked in for another two years.

They then looked at their budget for car servicing, but they knew in less than 12 months they would have another car to run while Oliver was at university. This was why they left the 'additional school fees' figure untouched. They knew the money would be needed elsewhere.

In the end, they decided to take $230 per fortnight from their Everyday Account and increase the direct debit to their Fixed Bills Account by $5,980 annually. This would leave them with only about $890 (rounded) per fortnight for the whole family to spend on things like buying clothes, petrol and takeaways. And if something broke, the associated expense would have to be paid from the Everyday Account.

They weren't sure if they were pushing themselves too far, but they decided to commit to this for six months and see how they went. After all, it would not be long before Oliver could get a job and work for his own 'having fun' money.

Once Oliver finished school, Grant and Wendy would commit $19,990 toward the home loan as extra repayments (about $769 per fortnight).

Grant and Wendy applied Winning Numbers 4 and 10 in order to achieve Winning Number 55 (i.e., their goal of paying off their home loan by the time Grant is 55):

- They are now using each of the 4 strategies to pay off their home loan faster.
- They got a better deal from their lender, saving 0.30% in interest.
- They already pay fortnightly, but this year will also make extra fortnightly repayments to their home loan with their combined savings in school fees, a reduction in discretionary spending and insurance premium savings.
- They have linked their savings account to their home loan. Once the credit card is paid off, they will build up their emergency savings until $55,000 is saved and offset against their home loan.

Grant and Wendy then apply the final **Winning Number: 120.**

They look at how their super funds are invested. They are both invested in the default Balanced Investment options for their respective funds. Wendy takes her age from 120 and gets 78, Grant takes his age from 120 and gets 76. They then look at the investment options they have available.

Neither of them wants to have complicated portfolios. They just want one simple investment option that pre-mixes the different assets together, and ensures they are diversified.

They both decide that their current Balanced Investment options remain the most suitable for them, given the investment choices they have to choose from.

Personal insurance and estate planning

Grant and Wendy note that neither of them has completed binding nomination forms for their super funds. They print off the respective forms from their fund websites, take them to work and get their colleagues to witness their signatures. Grant makes Wendy his binding death benefit beneficiary and Wendy makes Grant hers.

They decide to go to a licensed financial planner who specialises in personal insurance.

The adviser informs Wendy that she will not be able to get trauma (also called critical illness) insurance because of her medical history. Not only has she had breast cancer herself, but her mother did as well. Her family history combined with her own medical history represents too much risk to the insurer.

The adviser also informs Wendy that any new personal insurance for additional income protection and TPD cover would have a cancer exclusion. In other words, they would provide her with income protection and TPD insurance, but she would not be able to claim on the additional cover for not being able to work in the future due to cancer. This is because it is a pre-existing condition that will be applied, if the additional new cover is taken out.

Both Grant and Wendy are disappointed. The only consolation is that Wendy still has her existing insurances in place.

The adviser strongly recommended she keep her existing insurance cover in place because it has no cancer exclusion: the cover was in place before she was diagnosed with cancer.

Grant is eligible to apply for all four types of personal insurance (income protection, trauma, life and TPD), as he has no existing medical conditions.

He mentions to the adviser that the amount of life and TPD insurance cover that he and Wendy have inside super is falling every year. The adviser explains that this is common with default insurance held inside industry super funds.

Super fund members are allocated a certain number of units of cover. The dollar value of the cover applied to each unit falls as they get older.

The adviser recommends all four types of personal insurance cover for Grant to replace his existing insurance. Once the new, higher-quality insurance is in place, he will cancel his old policy.

The adviser also recommends a suite of personal insurance to complement Wendy's existing cover. While the new cover will not cover her for cancer, it will help to financially protect her against other life risks.

All their personal insurances (except Grant's trauma cover) will be held inside their super funds. As super funds no longer offer new cover for trauma insurance, Grant will pay the monthly premium for his trauma cover from their Fixed Expenses Account. There is a sufficient buffer in this account to absorb the cost.

Grant and Wendy understand that the additional insurances will impact their super retirement savings. However, when their home loan balance is lower, and the children have left home, they will review their insurance needs again.

Finally, Grant and Wendy make an appointment with a solicitor to have a full review of their estate planning. They will include a guardian for their children plus provisions for the establishment of a testamentary trust.

Grant and Wendy find an old photo of them at the beach in Phuket, Thailand on a holiday. They make a copy of it and write "our retirement" on it before putting it on the fridge. They also get the kids to each find a car they want to have (within their $15,000 budget) and print a picture of it. They write "Oliver's Car" and "Amelia's Car" on each photo and put them on the fridge as well.

Money will be tight, and they won't be having a holiday this year. But now they will see what they are saving for every time they use the fridge.

Grant and Wendy estimate that, at this stage by applying The Seven Winning Numbers, they will achieve the following:

1. They will pay the home loan off before Grant turns age 60, and save over $180,000 in interest.
2. They will save up for the purchase of a car for each of their children, rather than increasing their home loan debt to cover the cost.
3. They will clear their credit card debt, and reduce their reliance on credit to fund everyday items.
4. They will build a savings fund for emergencies, and use their additional savings to help reduce their home loan faster.

5. They will have more appropriate personal insurance in place, so that if something happens to them, they will be better protected financially.
6. Using the Moneysmart Superannuation Calculator[33], Grant estimates that he will have over $800,000 in super when he turns 62.
7. Using the Moneysmart Superannuation Calculator, Wendy estimates that she will have around $785,000 in super when she turns age 60.
8. Therefore, combined they estimate that they will have $1,585,000 in super to fund their retirement.

Wendy hasn't stopped living life for the now. But instead of going out for coffee or lunch with friends, she invites them over to her home instead. In doing so, she cuts the cost of socialising right down. Wendy still lives life for today, but at the same time saves and plans for her life of fun tomorrow, fun she knows she can afford.

EPILOGUE: SLEEPWALKING

> *"Sometimes people don't want to hear the truth because they don't want their illusions destroyed."*
>
> — Friedrich Nietzsche (19th century German philosopher)

You have just finished *The Seven Winning Numbers*, and now it is time to stop and reflect.

If you read the entire contents of this book and you do nothing with your finances, then you have actually done something. You have made a decision about your financial future by default – whether you realise it or not.

If you believe that the direction you are heading in with your money is not the right one and you do nothing to rectify this, only you will pay the price. No one else will. You are sleepwalking into financial mediocrity, and you will end up poorer than you should.

Money does not guarantee happiness, but a lack of money can be detrimental to our happiness. No one wants to have financial stress and worry in their lives.

Take control of your financial future. Ensure that you are rewarded financially for all of your hard work. Position yourself financially, so that you can get the most out of life. Do not let a lack of money hold you back from doing the things in life that you enjoy.

I believe that, if you apply The Seven Winning Numbers to your financial life early enough, you will achieve financial success, even if you earn an average income.

I also believe that should you then continue to manage your wealth wisely, you can also continue to enjoy your financial success throughout your retirement.

The best person to look after you when you are old, is you when you are young. No one can take better care of you financially, than you.

Secure your financial future during your working life, not by playing the lotto, not by leaving it to chance, but through deliberate, sensible actions you take when managing your money.

Always remember this:

If you bet on The Seven Winning Numbers, what are the odds of those numbers coming up?

1 in 1!

CONCLUSION

For many people, reading this book will be part of their continued quest to acquire as much wisdom as they can about wealth creation. They want to get ahead and make good decisions about their money, and are willing to do whatever is necessary to secure their financial position before they run out of time.

This type of person has realised that we get old faster than we get wise.

Similarly, they are also willing to pay for good financial advice. They do not see it as a cost, but as an investment in its own right: an investment toward a secure financial future.

There are, on the other hand, people who have very little interest in money. They go through life sleepwalking into financial uncertainty or failure. Eventually, they may realise (too late) that their retirement is restrictive, and funded mostly by government benefits.

These same sleepwalkers will be quite happy to spend $2,000 on a nice new couch for example, because they have decided that the old one is looking a little haggard. At the same time, they would never consider spending $2,000 on good financial advice. Even if that advice was guaranteed to be profoundly beneficial to them.

This may be because they do not trust advisors, or that they simply do not see the value in such an expense. Maybe it is because the benefits of a new couch can be enjoyed immediately. But it can take many years before they see the benefits from applying sound financial principles.

I hope that those of you who are proactively seeking financial knowledge and wisdom, find what you are looking for in this book, and secure a great financial future for yourselves and your family.

For those who have not been proactive in managing their financial futures or who have not been prepared to spend any money on good financial advice, I hope that someone hands them a copy of this book, and they consider applying The Seven Winning Numbers to their financial lives.

Maybe then they can have their couch and eat it too.

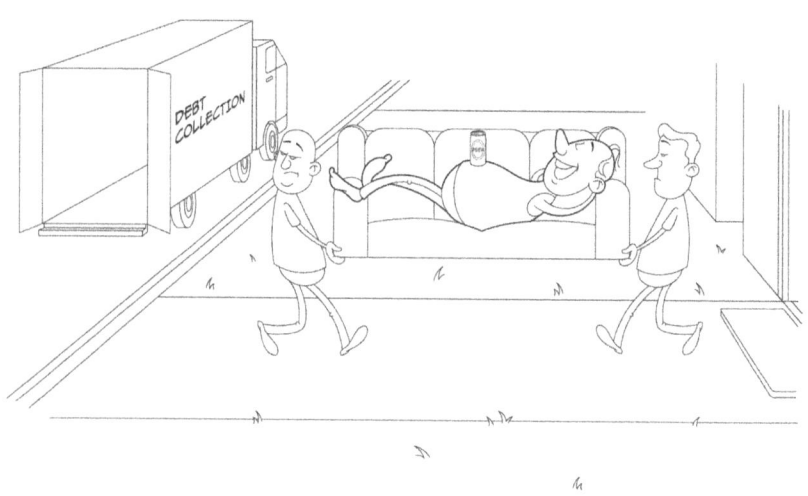

"THE COUCH WAS MONEY WELL SPENT!"

HELPFUL WEBSITES AND RESOURCES

ASIC Moneysmart

www.moneysmart.com.au

This is a broad and comprehensive site run by ASIC (the Australian Securities and Investments Commission, Australia's financial regulator). The site not only has information about most financial matters important to you, but it also has calculators and examples on how to do things like budgeting, investing and contributing more to super.

Moneysmart is an excellent website and should be your go-to before making any financial decisions.

Services Australia

www.servicesaustralia.gov.au/managing-your-money

Like Moneysmart, this is another government website that provides valuable information on financial matters, including calculators that will help you manage your money. Click on the 'Manage your Money' box on the site for tips on budgeting, dealing with debt and more.

Good Shepherd

www.goodshep.org.au

If you are a woman and struggling financially, you will find this website useful to source information and help. They offer counselling, financial support, loans and accommodation.

Cancer Council

www.cancer.org.au/support-and-services/practical-and-financial-assistance

The Cancer Council offers support to those that have suffered (or are suffering from) cancer. Their support includes helping you to get in touch with organisations that provide financial counselling at no cost, as well as bill assistance with utility providers.

SUPPORTING THE ENVIRONMENT

As a father, I not only worry about my son's financial future, I also worry about his future in general.

As humans, we consider ourselves to be the most intelligent species alive today.

Yet, we are the only species that poses the greatest risk to our own existence.

We talk about being carbon neutral, and even capturing the carbon we produce in order to fend off climate change. That thought process is tunneled. I believe we should do more than just that.

After all, how is it moral to plant fast-growing pine trees to capture carbon where koala habitat once stood? The koala habitat was already capturing carbon anyway via eucalypts, and it also happened to be teeming with native wildlife.

I believe there is a better way.

For every copy of *The Seven Winning Numbers* **purchased in any format, 5% of net profits will go to the Bush Heritage Australia Trust.**

Bush Heritage Australia is a charity whose mission is to purchase, protect and restore natural habitat in Australia.[34]

The Bush Heritage Australia Trust:

1. purchases degraded habitat and restores it back to its natural state. This is achieved by eliminating invasive species, allowing native species to flourish once again as well as conducting native species planting programs.
2. partners with aboriginal groups in order to work with them to deliver conservation outcomes on native title land.
3. collaborates with private landholders, communities and other conservation groups across Australia, in order to deliver conservation outcomes above and beyond what the Trust could do by itself.

Bush Heritage Australia aims to preserve our flora and fauna, and protect them from becoming extinct. In doing so, they also happen to capture carbon naturally and sustainably.

Bringing native plants and animals back from the brink of extinction, while capturing carbon at the same time, is the better way.

We can combat the destructive impact we have on the environment, and help protect the future of life on this planet and our ability to exist on it.

I hope my son (and one day, his children) can live not just on a healthy planet, but on an interesting one too. There is nothing like seeing the look in your son's eyes when he sees a koala or a kangaroo for the first time: the excitement, awe and wonder.

More about Bush Heritage Australia can be found here: www.bushheritage.org.au.

ENDNOTES

[1] https://thepfsa.co.uk/football-wages-how-much-do-footballers-get-paid/#:~:

[2] https://help.thelott.com/hc/en-us/articles/4422500461337-What-are-the-chances-of-winning-division-one-

[3] https://www.amp.com.au/home-loans/calculators/rapid-pay

[4] Ibid.

[5] https://www.ato.gov.au/individuals/super/in-detail/growing-your-super/super-contributions---too-much-can-mean-extra-tax/?page=2

[6] https://www.ato.gov.au/rates/individual-income-tax-rates/

[7] https://www.ato.gov.au/Individuals/Super/In-detail/Withdrawing-and-using-your-super/COVID-19-early-release-of-super-(closed-31-December-2020)/

[8] https://www.ato.gov.au/rates/key-superannuation-rates-and-thresholds/?anchor=Superguaranteepercentage#Superguaranteepercentage

[9] https://www.ato.gov.au/individuals/super/in-detail/growing-your-super/super-contributions---too-much-can-mean-extra-tax/?page=3#:~:

[10] https://moneysmart.gov.au/how-super-works/superannuation-calculator

[11] Ibid.

[12] https://www.vanguard.com.au/personal/invest-with-us/etf?portId=8205

[13] https://www.ato.gov.au/rates/changes-to-company-tax-rates/

[14] https://nucleuswealth.com/articles/about-those-australian-dividend-yields/

[15] https://www.afr.com/markets/equity-markets/australia-s-sharemarket-has-a-size-problem-20220802-p5b6ol

[16] https://en.wikipedia.org/wiki/List_of_stock_exchanges

[17] https://www.vanguard.com.au/institutional/products/en/detail/etf/8212/equity

[18] https://www.vanguard.com.au/adviser/products/en/detail/etf/8205/equity

[19] Ibid.

[20] https://www.vanguard.com.au/adviser/products/en/detail/etf/8205/equity

[21] https://www.canstar.com.au/investor-hub/australian-share-performance-30-years/

[22] https://www.amazon.com.au/Warren-Buffett-Interpretation-Financial-Statement/dp/1416573186

[23] https://www.ato.gov.au/rates/individual-income-tax-rates/

[24] https://www.statista.com/statistics/326707/bitcoin-price-index/

[25] https://www.ato.gov.au/rates/individual-income-tax-rates/

[26] https://www.ato.gov.au/individuals/super/in-detail/growing-your-super/super-contributions---too-much-can-mean-extra-tax/?anchor=Concessionalcontributionsandcontribution#Concessionalcontributionsandcontribution

[27] https://www.amp.com.au/home-loans/calculators/rapid-pay

[28] https://moneysmart.gov.au/how-super-works/superannuation-calculator

[29] https://www.ato.gov.au/Individuals/Medicare-and-private-health-insurance/Private-health-insurance-rebate/Lifetime-health-cover/

[30] https://www.ato.gov.au/individuals/medicare-and-private-health-insurance/medicare-levy-surcharge/

[31] https://www.amp.com.au/home-loans/calculators/rapid-pay

[32] https://www.amp.com.au/home-loans/calculators/rapid-pay

[33] https://moneysmart.gov.au/how-super-works/superannuation-calculator

[34] https://www.bushheritage.org.au/

www.ingramcontent.com/pod-product-compliance
Lightning Source LLC
Chambersburg PA
CBHW051536010526
44107CB00064B/2744